Viva

# Speed M



## Mental Maths Skills

# 4

A Parker
J Faulkner

VIVA EDUCATION

New Delhi • Bangalore • Chennai • Hyderabad • Kolkata • Mumbai

VIVA EDUCATION



First Published, 2007

**VIVA EDUCATION PRIVATE LIMITED**

- 4737/23, Ansari Road, Daryaganj, New Delhi 110 002
  E-mail: vivadelhi@vivagroupindia.net, Tel: 42242200
- Plot No. 76, Service Industries Shirvane, Sector 1, Nerul, Navi Mumbai 400 706
  E-mail: vivamumbai@vivagroupindia.net, Tel. 27721273, 27721274
- Jamals Fazal Chambers, 26 Greams Road, Chennai 600 006
  E-mail: vivachennai@vivagroupindia.net, Tel: 28294241, 2829304
- B-103, Jindal Towers, 21/1A/3 Darga Road, Kolkata 700 017
  E-mail: vivakolkata@vivagroupindia.net, Tel: 22816713
- 7, GF, Sovereign Park Apartments, 56-58, K. R. Road, Basavanagudi, Bangalore 560 004
  E-mail: vivabangalore@vivagroupindia.net, Tel: 26607409
- 101-102 Moghal Marc Apartments, 3-4-637 to 641, Narayanguda, Hyderabad 500 029
  E-mail: vivahyderabad@vivagroupindia.net, Tel: 27564481

  Visit us at www.vivagroupindia.com

*Published by arrangement with*

Pascal Educational Services
655 Parramatta Road
Leichhardt NSW 2040
Australia

Based on *Signpost Mental Maths* by A Parker and J Faulkner

Indian adaptation
Swati Duggal Chojer, Modern School, New Delhi.

ISBN 10 : 81-8327-109-X
ISBN 13 : 978-81-8327-109-7

Rs 72.00

Printed and bound at Sanat Printers, Kundli.

Time: 15 minutes

Score ________

# 1 Quiz - Time

**1.** Write the Standard numerals.

a. 40000 + 300 + 40 + 4 = ______

b. 93000 + 6000 + 50 + 8 = ______

c. 30000 + 4300 + 900 + 48 = ______

d. 42000 + 700 + 91 + 9 = ______

**2.** Fill in the blanks.

a. (8 x 6) – (4 x 6) = ______

b. ______ + 3 = 1427

c. ______ x 10 = 3400

d. 200 p = Rs ______

e. 1490 – 490 = ______

f. 9 dozens = ______

g. There are 1020 minutes in ______ hours.

h. Half of one and a half = ______

i. Triple 16 then halve ______

j. 5720 ÷ 20 = ______

**3.** Solve

a. (3 × 4) ÷ 3 + 5 = ______

b. (92 ÷ 2) + 223 = ______

c. (15 ÷ 3) + 17 = ______

d. (12 × 3) – 23 = ______

**4.** The cost of one pencil box is Rs 25, so the cost of 3 dozen pencil boxes will be ______

**5.** How many days are there between 18 April and 5 May? ________

**6.** Write all odd numbers between 507 and 521 ______________________________

**7.** Write the first 4 multiples of 11. ______________________________

**8.** There are 4800 eggs in 20 boxes, so each box has ______ eggs.

**9.** There are 4200 pencils in 30 boxes, so each box has ______ pencils.

**10.** The cricket team compared their batting scores. Tendulkar scored 30 less than Dravid, who had scored 15 more than Saurav. Saurav had made 95. What were the players' scores?

Tendulkar ______ Dravid ______

# ACTIVITY SHEET 1

Grade

**1.** Complete the following labels using mL or L.

**2.** Which temperature do these suggest: (high/low)?

a.  ______

b.  ______

c.  ______

d.  ______

e. The small finger of a 10 years old boy is about 15 cm (true / false). ______

**3.** Fill in the blanks.

a. The cost of 12 kg chops at Rs 50 a kilogram is ______

b. 600 g + 200 g = ______ g.

**4.** Complete each magic square.

a.

| | | |
|---|---|---|
| | | 12 |
| | 9 | |
| 6 | | 8 |

b.

| | | |
|---|---|---|
| 9 | 4 | |
| 2 | | 10 |
| 7 | | |

c.

| | | |
|---|---|---|
| 6 | 1 | |
| | | |
| 2 | 9 | 4 |

d.

| | | |
|---|---|---|
| 7 | | 5 |
| | 8 | |
| | | 9 |

e.

| | | |
|---|---|---|
| 11 | | 9 |
| | 12 | |
| | | 13 |

f.

| | | |
|---|---|---|
| | 13 | |
| | 11 | |
| 10 | 9 | |

Grade

# ACTIVITY SHEET 2

**1.** Use the information given to colour the pattern.

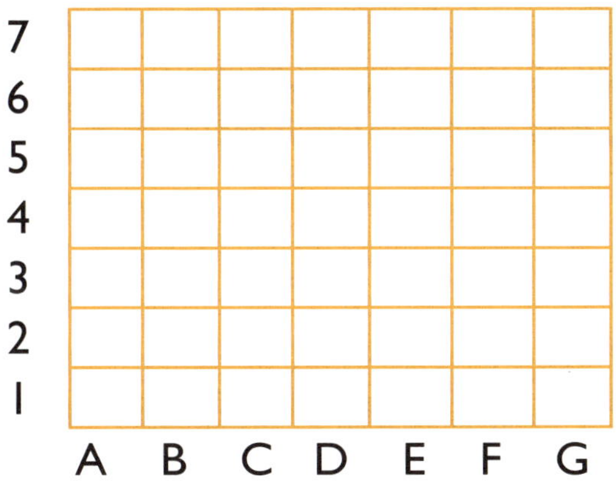


a. Colour green D4

b. Colour red C4, D3, D5, E4.

c. Colour blue B4, D2, D6, F4.

d. Colour yellow A4, B3, B5, C2, C6, D1, D7, E2, E6, F3, F5, G4.

e. Identify the shape which has been made by colouring the pattern. ________________

## A-Maze-Ing

Find the way through.

# ACTIVITY SHEET 3

Grade ☐

**1.** Measure the total length of each line to the nearest centimetre.

a.

a. ______

b.

b. ______

c.

c. ______

**2.** Match each plane shape with the correct label.

______

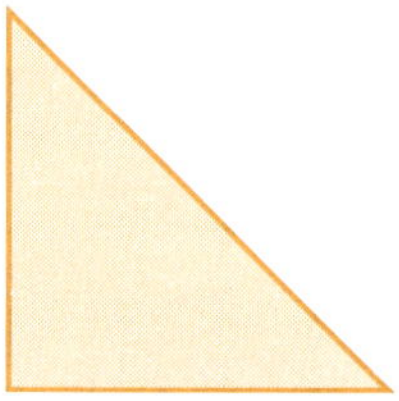

______

______

| | | |
|---|---|---|
| A 3 sides | B 4 equal sides | C 2 opposite sides of equal length |
| D 6 equal sides | E 5 equal sides | F 2 pairs of equal adjacent sides |

______

______

______

Grade

# ACTIVITY SHEET 4

**1.** Label these plane shapes.

a. ________

b. ________

c. ________

d. ________

e. ________

f. ________

g. ________

h. ________

**2.** Complete:

Look for the sign

| | + 5050 | |
|---|---|---|
| 150 | | 5200 |
| 322 | | |
| 423 | | |
| 880 | | |
| 2497 | | |
| 346 | | |
| 879 | | |
| 945 | | |
| 1187 | | |
| 241 | | |
| 422 | | |
| 199 | | |

| 7005 – | | |
|---|---|---|
| | 985 | 6020 |
| | 632 | |
| | 828 | |
| | 213 | |
| | 1569 | |
| | 123 | |
| | 487 | |
| | 1000 | |
| | 4223 | |
| | 132 | |
| | 297 | |
| | 784 | |

# ACTIVITY SHEET 5

Grade

**1.** Answer the following.

a. How many 25 p in Rs 20? ______

b. How many 50 p in Rs 100? ______

c. 150 ml + 50 ml = ______

d. Is milk measured in g or ml?______

e. Factors of 10 are ______

f. Years from 1980 to 1990 ______

g. Fifteen minutes before 11.00 a.m. is ______

h. Hours between 8.00 a.m. and 2.00 p.m. are ______

i. Weeks in 1 year ______

j. Months in 10 years ______

k. The multiples of 8 less than 40 are ____________________________

l. The number ______ is a common factor of all numbers.

**2.** Record the temperature shown on each thermometer.

a. b. c. d.

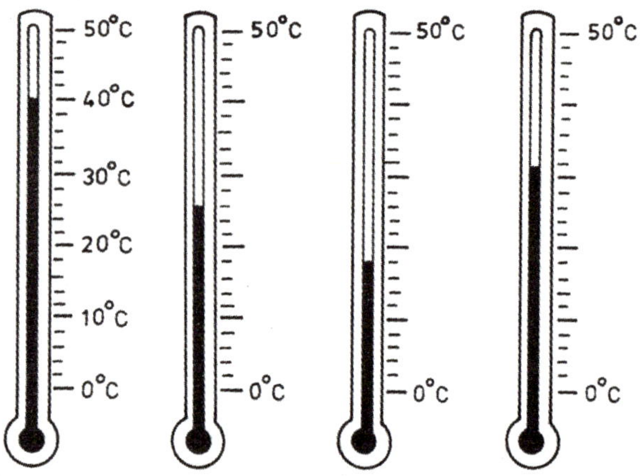


a. ______ b. ______

c. ______ d. ______

**3.** Mark the given temperature.

a. b. c. d.

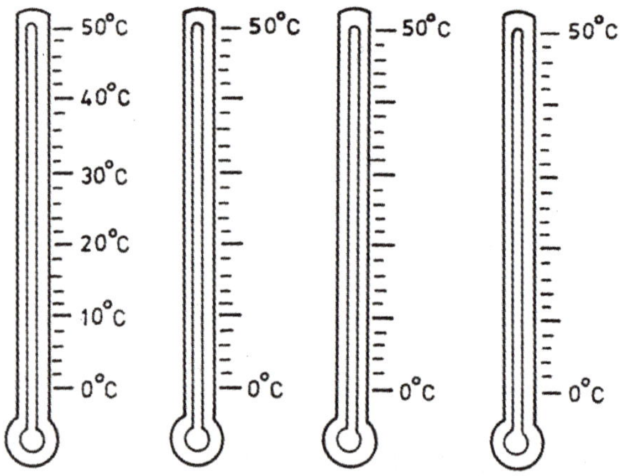


a. 38 °C b. 28 °C

c. 10 °C d. 47 °C

**4.** The silver liquid inside a thermometer is called ________

Grade

# ACTIVITY SHEET 6

**1.** Read the abacus and write the number for each.

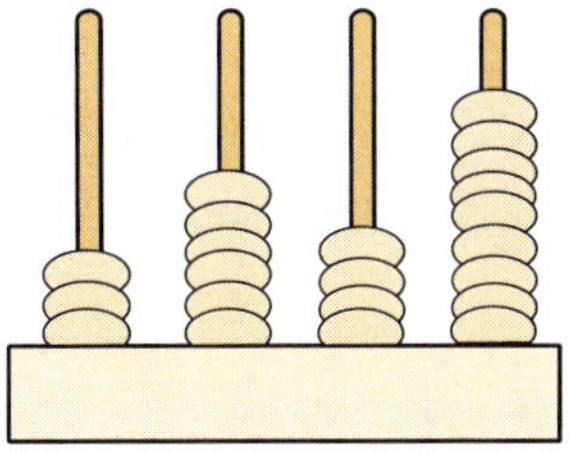

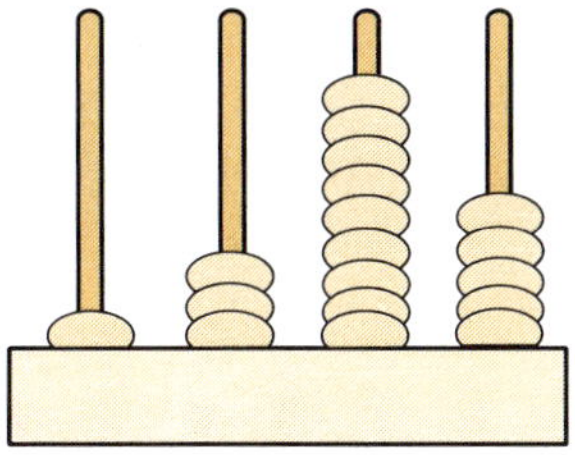

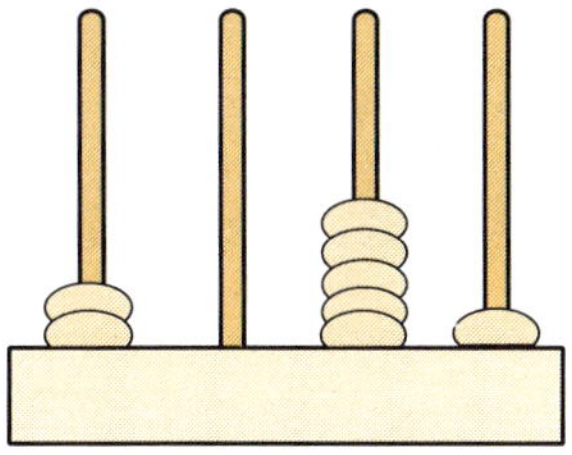

a. __________ b. __________ c. __________

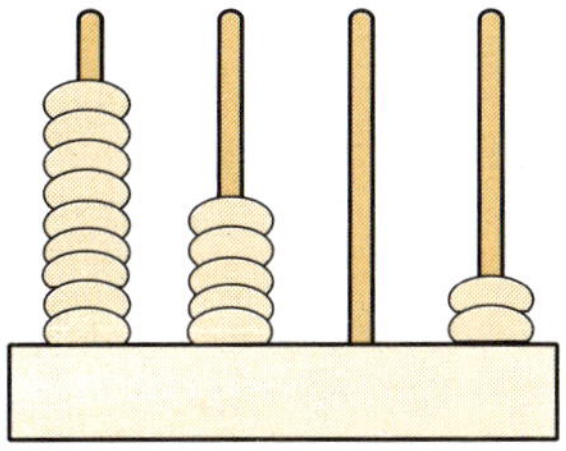

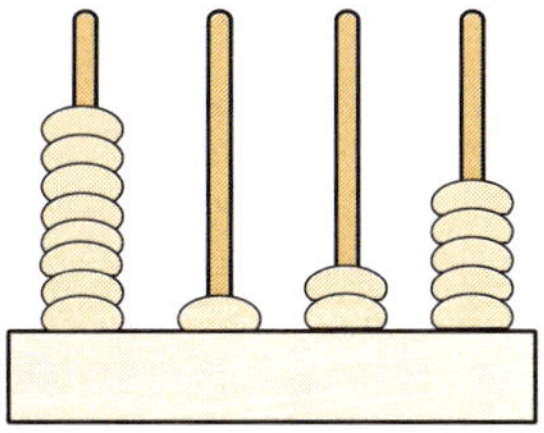

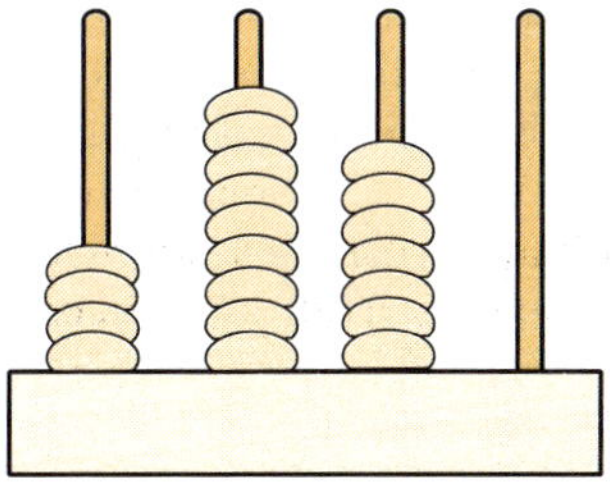

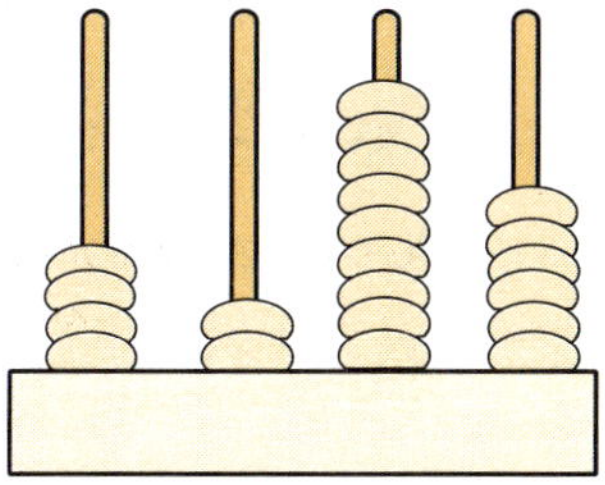

d. __________ e. __________ f. __________ g. __________

**2.** Estimate the length of each line. Find a way to check your answer.

a. Estimate: ______ cm

Check: ______ cm

b. Estimate: ______ cm

Check: ______ cm

# ACTIVITY SHEET 7

Grade

**1.** Answer the following.

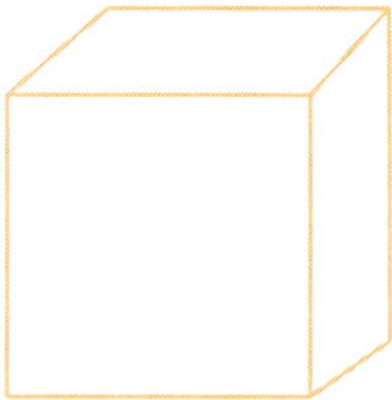

a. Name this shape ________

b. Name an object that looks like this shape. ________

c. Is cube a solid or a plane shape? ________

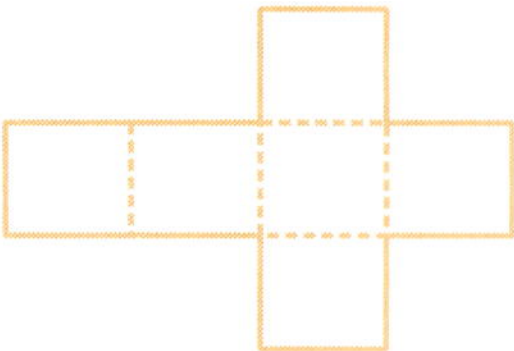

d. This is the net of a ________

e. How many corners has a cube? ________

f. A cube has ________ edges.

g. Would cubes stack easily? ________

h. A cube has ________ faces.

i. Show 15 minutes before midnight and 15 minutes after noon.

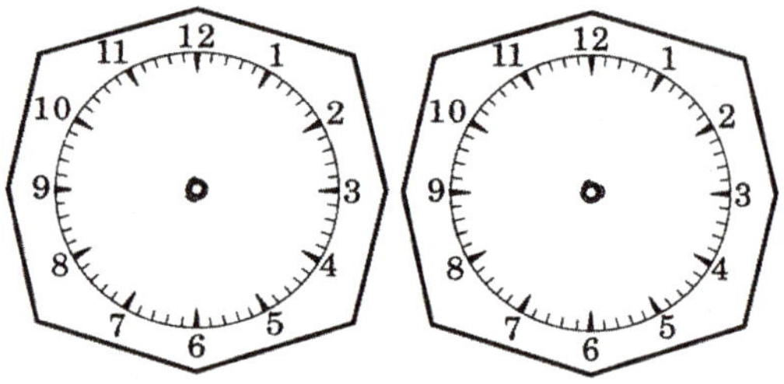


**2.** What fraction of each shape is shaded?

a.

b.

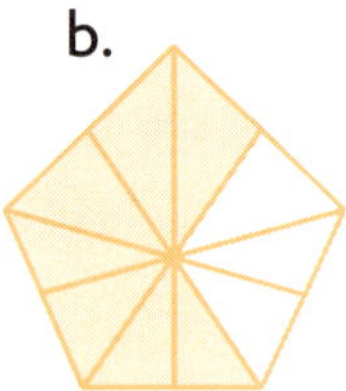

c.

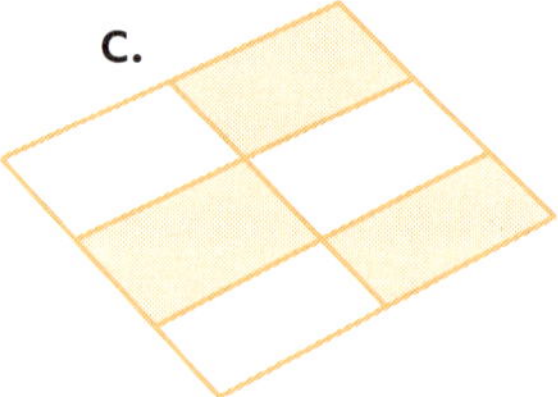

d.

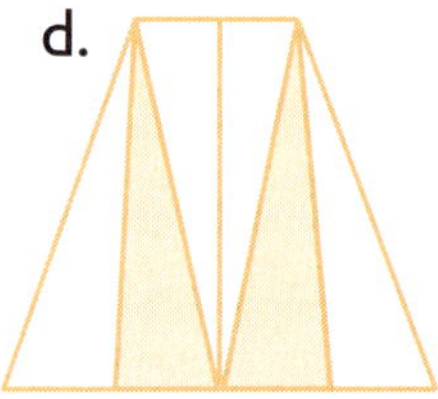

e.

**3.** Shade part of each shape to match the fraction given.

a.



$\frac{6}{8}$

b.

$\frac{4}{5}$

c.



$\frac{3}{8}$

d.

$\frac{4}{10}$

e.

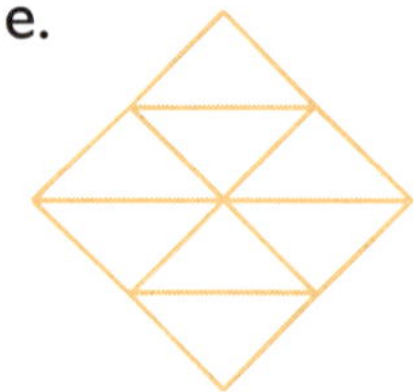

$\frac{5}{8}$

Grade

# ACTIVITY SHEET 8

**1.** Find the perimeter and the area of these shapes and complete the table. Each small square is of 1 cm side.

Perimeter is the distance around the shape

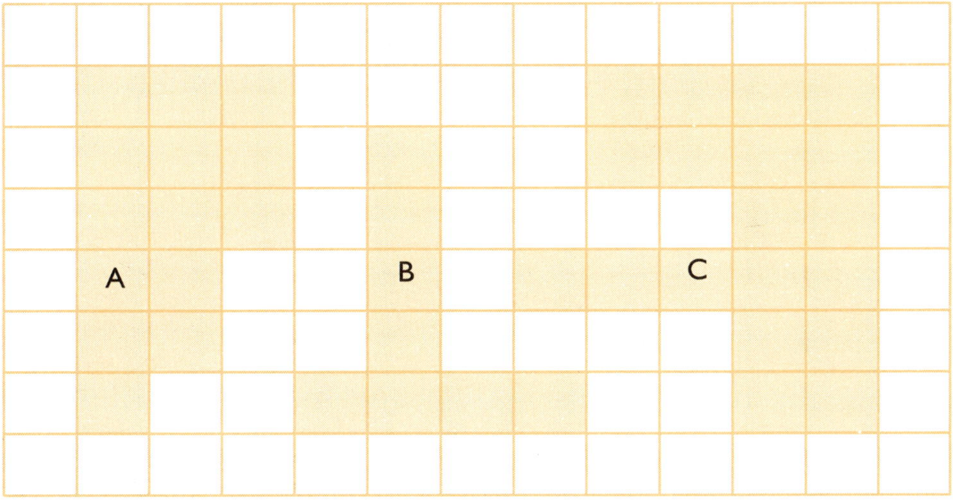


| | Perimeter | Area |
|---|---|---|
| A | cm | $cm^2$ |
| B | cm | $cm^2$ |
| C | cm | $cm^2$ |

**2.** Answer the following.

a. Four packets each have a mass of 450 g. What is the total mass in kilograms? ______

b. How many days are there from 19th September to 18th October? ______

c. It is 15 °C at 7.00 a.m. and 33 °C at 3.00 p.m. By how much has the temperature risen? ______

d. Write the number for one thousand five hundred and thirty-seven. ______

e. Thirty people each have Rs 3000. How much do they have altogether?

______

f. Separate 64 roses into 8 equal bunches. How many in each bunch? ______

g. I spent Rs 100 at the fruit shop and Rs 150 at the supermarket.
How much did I spend altogether? ______
How much change from Rs 500? ______

h. Sam has 3 dozen pencils and Tony has $2\frac{1}{2}$ dozen pencils. How many altogether? ______

i. Is 4890 smaller than 4980? (yes/no) ______

# ACTIVITY SHEET 9

Grade ☐

**1.** Complete these webs.

a.

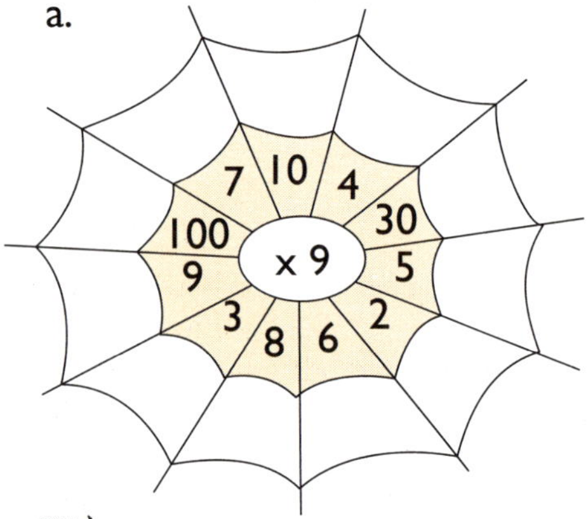


b.

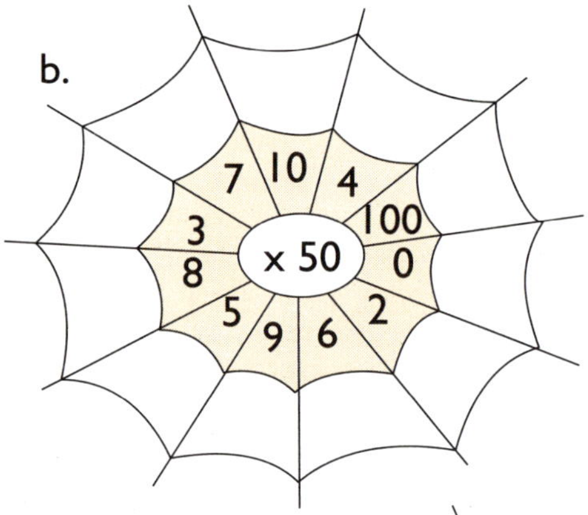

c.

d.

**2.** Miss Roberts kept this tally of Class 4 scores on a half-yearly Spelling test.

a. How many children scored:

(i) 11-20 marks ______

(ii) less than 21 ______

(iii) more than 20 ______

(iv) more than 30 ______

(v) more than 10 ______

(vi) less than 31 ______

Tally of Class 4 results

| Words correct | | | | | |
|---|---|---|---|---|---|
| 1 to 10 | 𝍸 | \| | | | |
| 11 to 20 | 𝍸 | 𝍸 | \|\|\| | | |
| 21 to 30 | 𝍸 | 𝍸 | 𝍸 | 𝍸 | \|\|\| |
| 31 to 40 | 𝍸 | 𝍸 | 𝍸 | \|\| | |

b. How many students in Class 4? ______

c. How many words in the test? ______

# ACTIVITY SHEET 10

**1.** Complete these factor wheels.

Prime numbers have themselves and one as factors

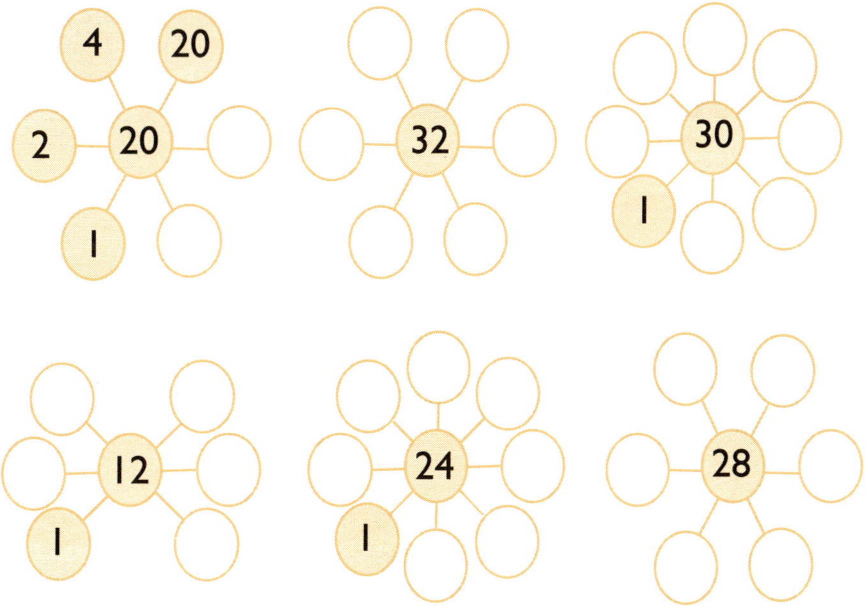


**2.** Add the correct unit of measure for each of the following.

**3.** How many packages make 1 kg?

a. Soap ______ b. Cheesies ______

c. Cocoa ______ d. Choc Chip cookies ______

# ACTIVITY SHEET 11

Grade

**1.** Colour the various shapes that tessellate.

a.
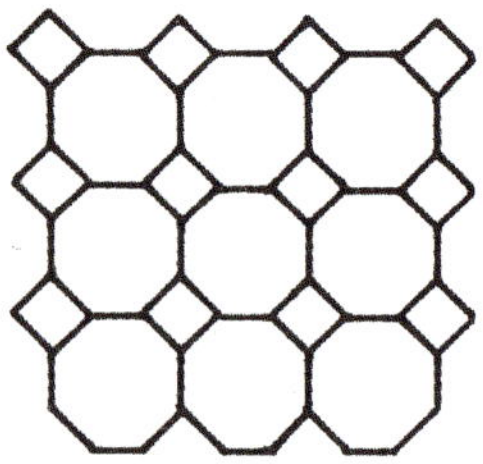

b.

c.
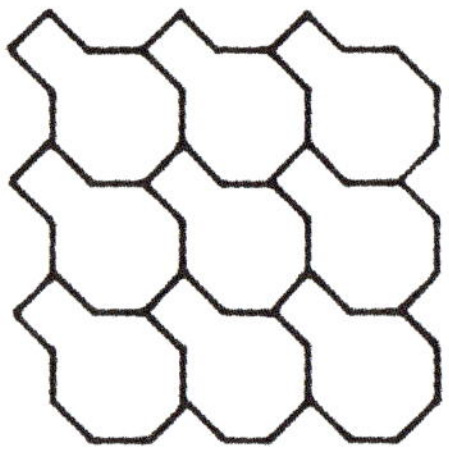

d.
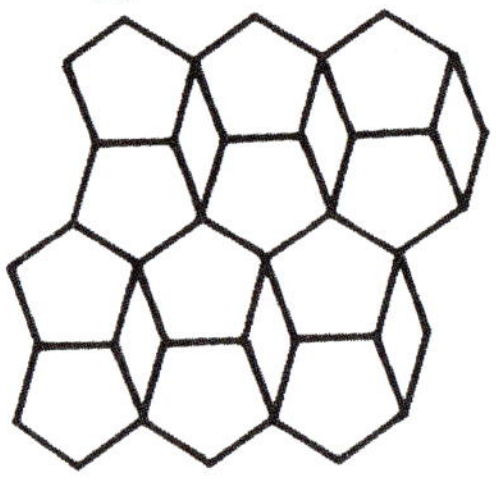

e.

f.
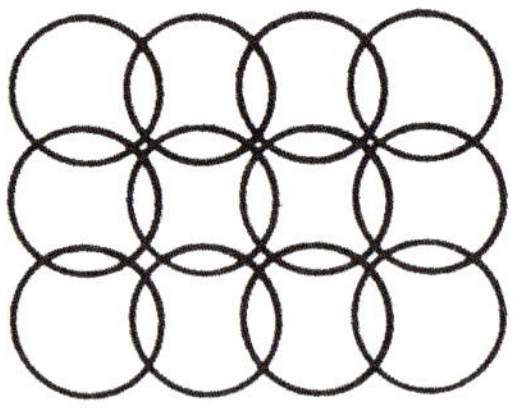

g.
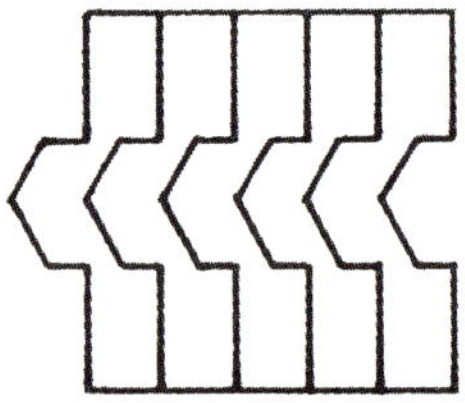

h.
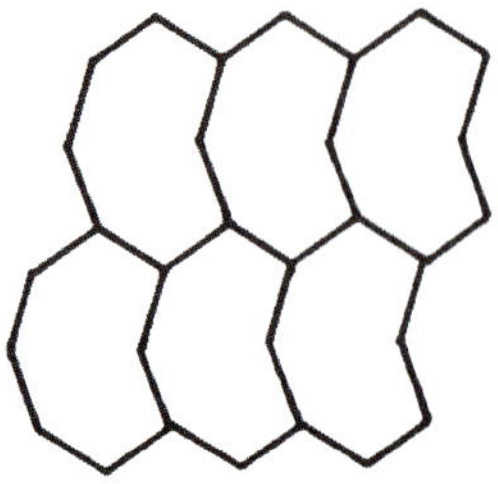

**2.** Answer the following.

a. How many 6's make 54? ______

b. Total of 5 tens and 3 tens ______

c. 2 minutes after 25 to 9 is [ : ]

d. Mass of an apple is ______ than 1 kg.

e. Mass of a pumpkin is ______ than 1 kg.

f. Write the smallest number using 2, 6, 4, 9 ______

g. Write the largest number using 3, 7, 5, 8 ______

h. Write the set of factors for 30 ______

i. Dolly was 10 years old in 1983. How old will she be at the end of 1996? ______

j. How many legs altogether on six spiders? ______

k. Total number of days in February and March in a leap year ______

l. 1 kg of feathers is lighter than a kg of sand. (true/false) ______

**3.** Find the perimeter.

______

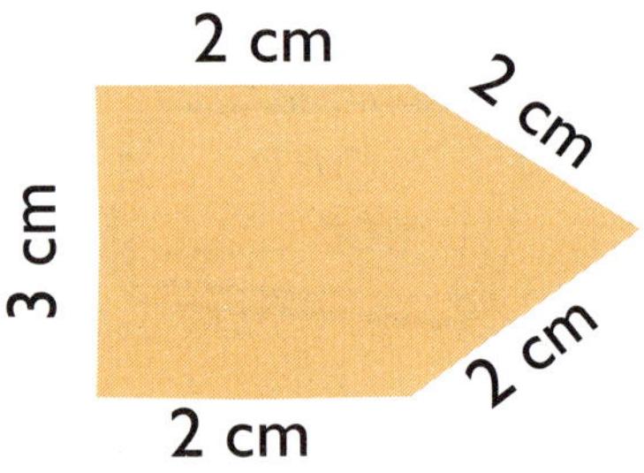

Grade

# ACTIVITY SHEET 12

Test your speed.

How many can you complete in each set in two minutes?

Score

**1.** a. ______ m = 1 km    b. 1 kg = ______ g

c. ______ ml = 14 l    d. 1/2 km = ______ m

e. ______ cm = 1 m    f. 500 m = ______ km

g. ______ ml = 1/2 l    h. 1/2 m = ______ cm

i. ______ p = 1 Re    j. 500 g = ______ kg

**2.** a. $5^2$ = ______    b. 10 × 5 = ______    c. 25 ÷ 5 = ______

d. 3 × 5 = ______    e. 5 × 8 = ______    f. 45 ÷ 5 = ______

g. 50 ÷ 5 = ______    h. 2 × 5 = ______    i. 4 × 5 = ______

j. 15 ÷ 5 = ______    k. 35 ÷ 5 = ______    l. 6 × 5 = ______

m. 8 × 5 = ______    n. 40 ÷ 5 = ______    o. 10 ÷ 5 = ______

p. 7 × 5 = ______    q. 5 × 5 = ______    r. 30 ÷ 5 = ______

s. 20 ÷ 5 = ______    t. 100 × 5 = ______    u. 25 × 1 = ______

**3.** a. $3^2$ = ______    b. 3 ÷ 3 = ______    c. 2 × 3 = ______

d. 30 ÷ 3 = ______    e. 6 × 3 = ______    f. 7 × 3 = ______

g. 9 × 3 = ______    h. 12 ÷ 3 = ______    i. 20 × 3 = ______

j. 3 × 3 = ______    k. 21 ÷ 3 = ______    l. 18 ÷ 3 = ______

m. 3 + 3 + 3 = ______    n. 5 × 3 = ______    o. 8 × 3 = ______

p. 9 ÷ 3 = ______    q. 6 ÷ 3 = ______    r. 4 × 3 = ______

s. 100 × 3 = ______    t. 15 ÷ 3 = ______    u. 24 ÷ 3 = ______

v. 10 × 3 = ______    w. 27 ÷ 3 = ______

# ACTIVITY SHEET 13

Grade

Read the temperature-time graph and answer the following questions.

**1.** The time when the temperature was:

a. 25 °C _______

b. 22 °C _______

c. 29 °C _______

**2.** The temperature at:

a. 9 a.m. _______

b. 1 p.m. _______

c. 5 p.m. _______

**3.** The change in temperature between 12 noon and 4 p.m. _______

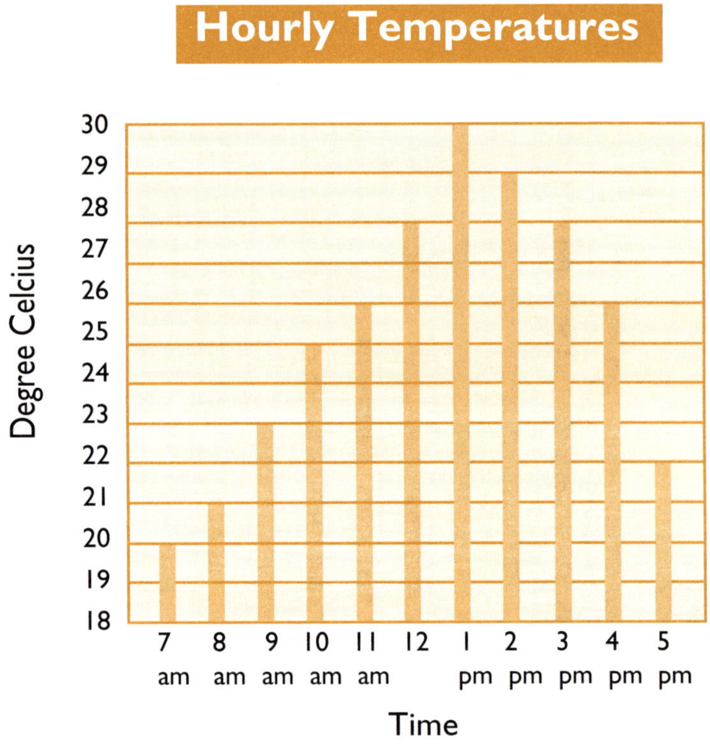


**4.** Use your imagination to make a circular design which includes all the plane shapes you have studied so far. Colour your design.

Grade □

# ACTIVITY SHEET 14

**1.** Make the largest possible number from:

a. 4, 2, 5 __________  b. 7, 0, 9 __________

**2.** Total number of:

a. days in 2 weeks ______  b. seconds in 3 minutes ______

c. months in autumn ______  d. months in $12\frac{1}{2}$ years ______

**3.** What is the time in a digital clock:

a. 15 minutes before midnight ______  b. 10 minutes before 7 ______

c. 18 minutes after mid-day ______  d. 4 minutes after 7:58 ______

**4.** Colour the fraction:

a. 2 / 3 □ □ □  b. 4 / 5 □ □ □ □ □

c. 5 / 6 □ □ □ □ □ □  d. 1 / 2 □ □

**5.** Draw axis of symmetry in the given shapes.

**6.** List the factors of:

a. 12 __________  b. 14 __________  c. 16 __________

d. 18 __________  e. 20 __________  f. 24 __________

7. Find the perimeter of the given shape.

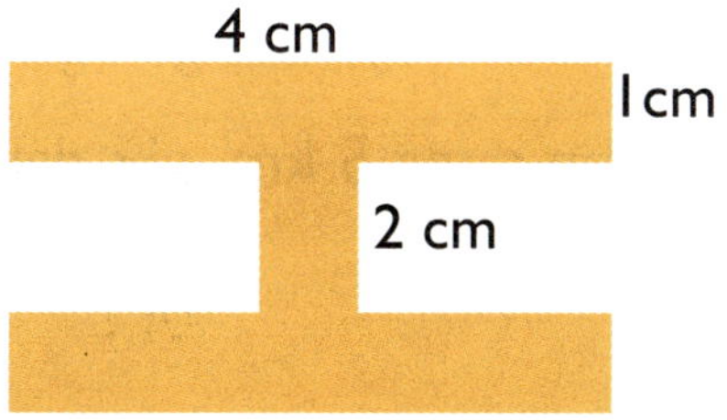


__________

# ACTIVITY SHEET 15

Grade

**1.** Complete the webs. One has been done for you.

a.

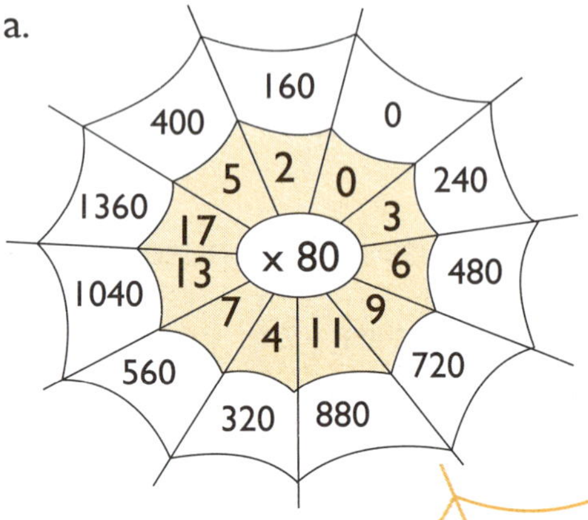


b.

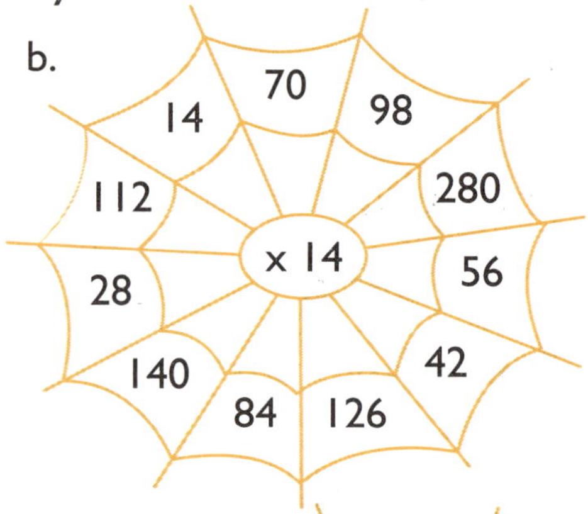

c.

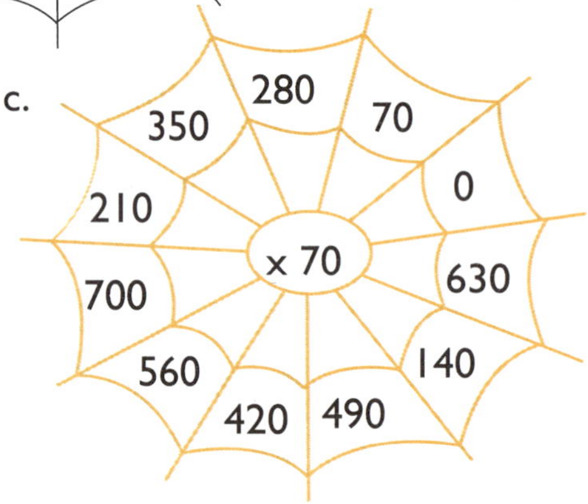


d.

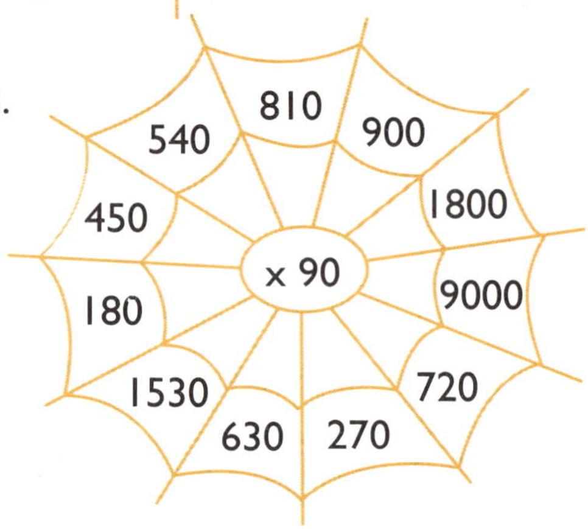


**2.** Answer the following.

a. Write 2304 in expanded notation. ______________________________

b. Hindu-Arabic numeral for LXVII ______________________________

c. Round off 367 to the nearest ten ______________________________

d. One kilogram of pumpkin is cut into 4 equal pieces. What is the mass of each piece? ______

e. Perimeter of a square with a 5 m side ______

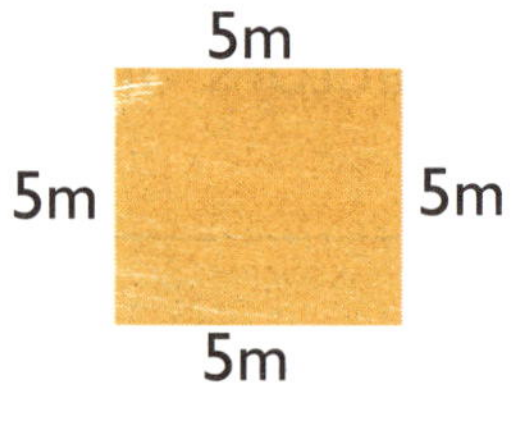


f. How many 100 g sugar-bags would balance a 500 g sugar-bag? ______

g. John runs 5 km, six days a week. How far does he run eack week? ______

Grade

# ACTIVITY SHEET 16

**1.** Show each time on the clock face.

a.
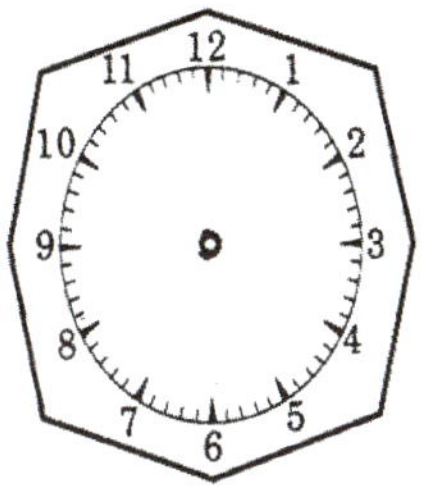
7:15

b.
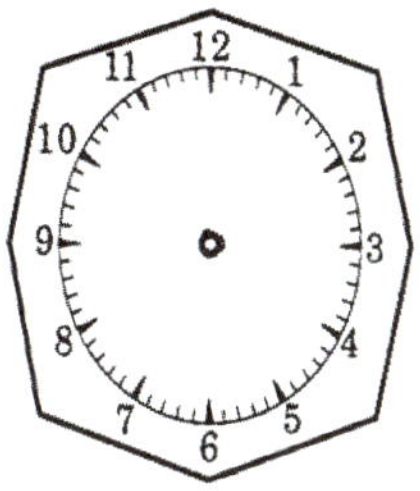
9:00

c.
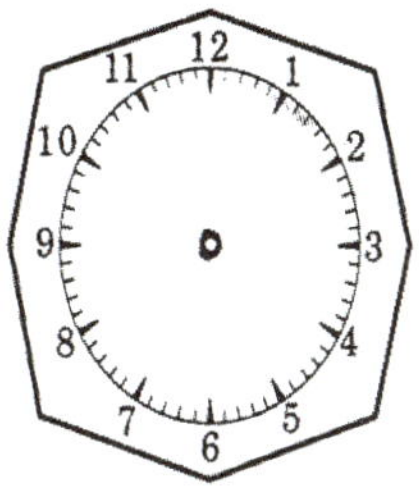
4:30

d.
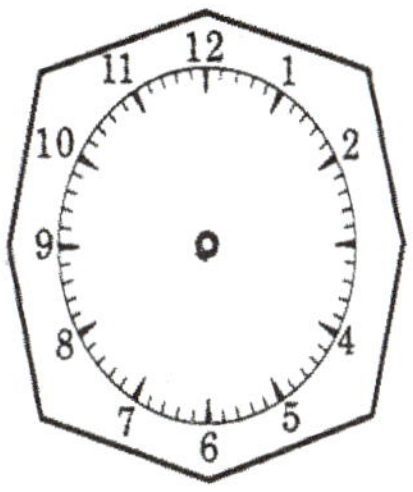
11:50

e.
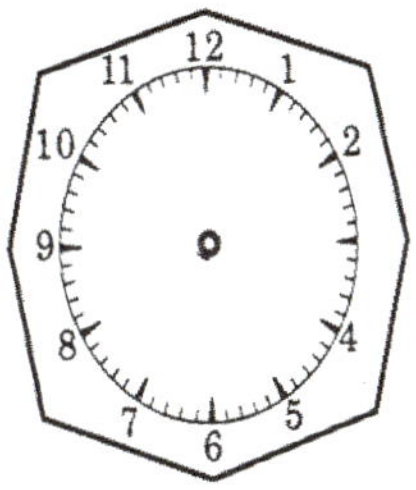
8:20

f.
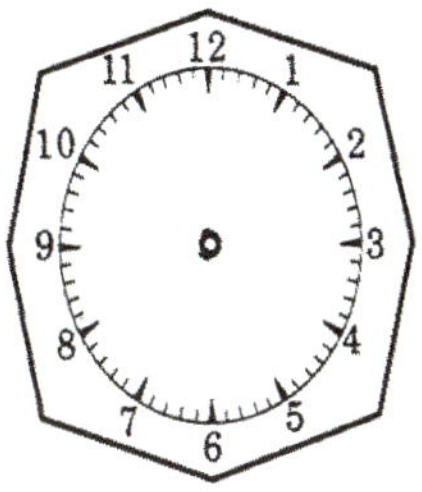
6:45

g.
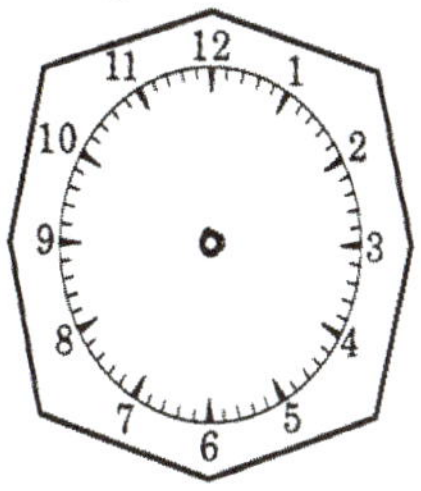
12:00

h.
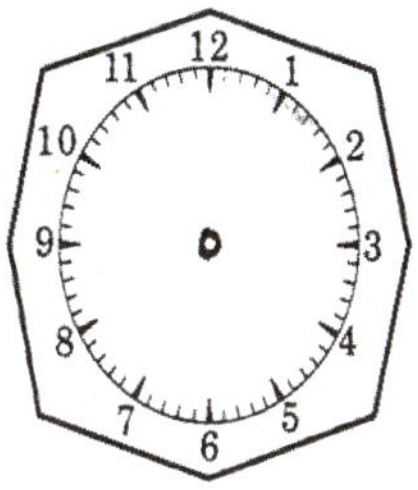
5:10

i.
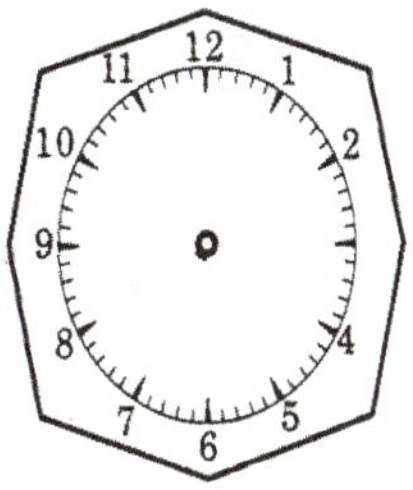
3:35

j.
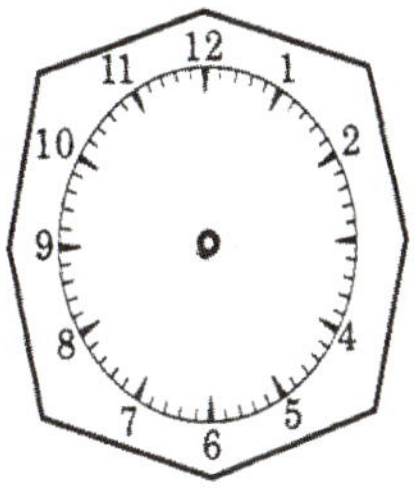
2:25

**2.** Read the graph and answer the following.

a. Which club has the most members? _______

b. Which club has the least members? _______

c. How many members of

Swimming _______

Badminton _______

d. How many more members in Soccer than in Golf? _______

e. Which clubs have equal members? _______

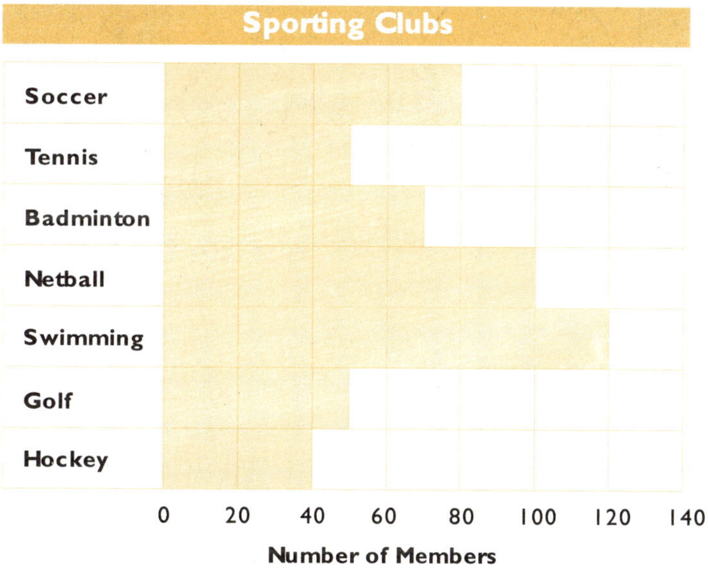

# ACTIVITY SHEET 17

Grade ☐

**1.** Fill in the blanks.

a. The next odd number after 93 is ______

b. mL in 1 litre ______

c. Seconds in 3 minutes = ______

d. Area is measured in ______

e. 40 tens make ______ hundreds

f. Ten minutes before 3.00 a.m. is ______

g. The cost of 1.5 kg of carrots at Rs 15 a kilogram = Rs ______

h. What is the cost of $3\frac{1}{2}$ dozen pencils, if six pencils cost Rs 4? ______

i. The height of this book is about (15 cm /30 cm /60 cm). ______

j. What is the perimeter of a book which is of 20 cm width and 30 cm length? ______

l. Could the weight of a woman be 65 g? (yes/no) ______

m. Abhishek works 3 hours daily at Rs 75 an hour. Calculate his total earnings for one week. ______

**2.** Show these times in the analog and the digital form.

a.

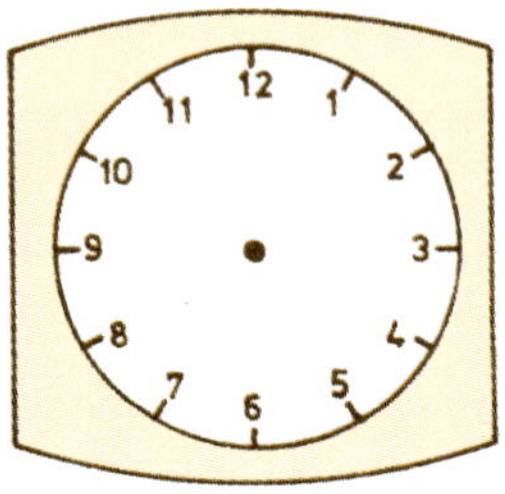

half past 11

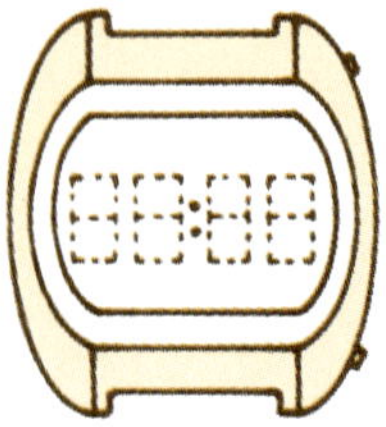

b.

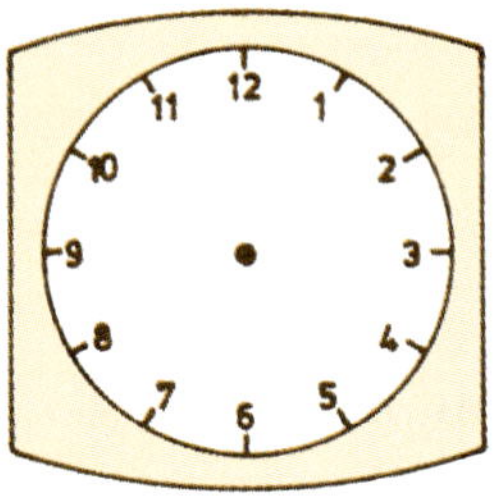

quarter past 7

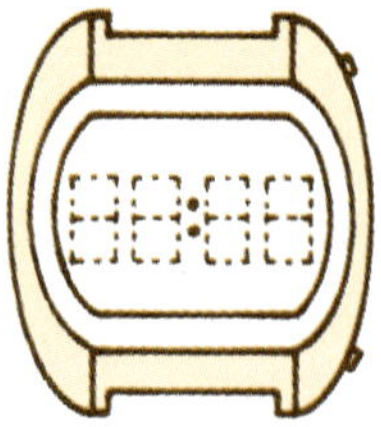

c.

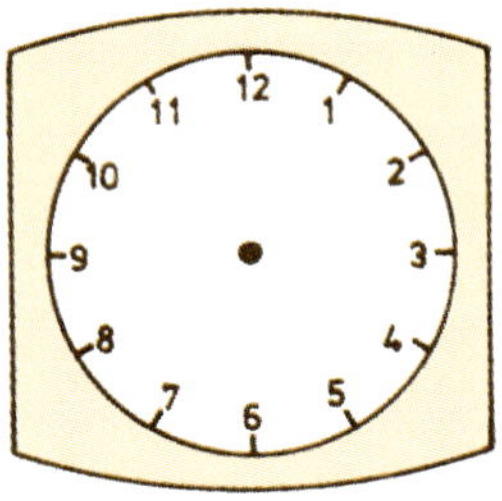

4 o'clock

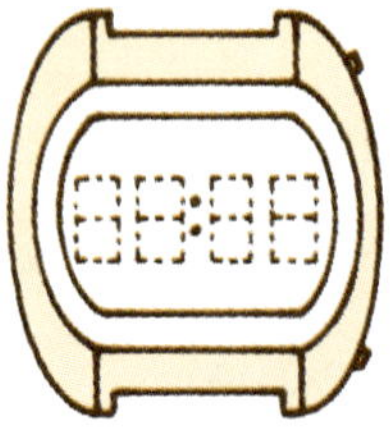

d.

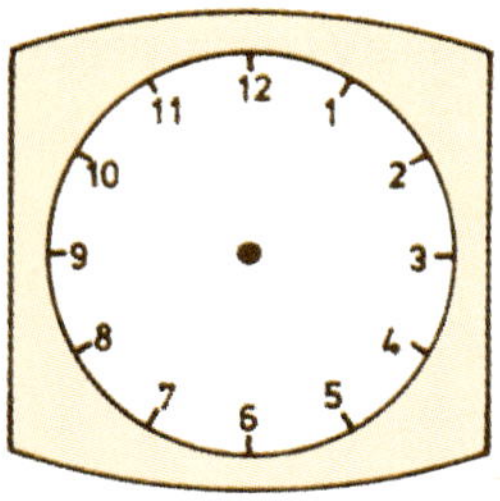

quarter to 5

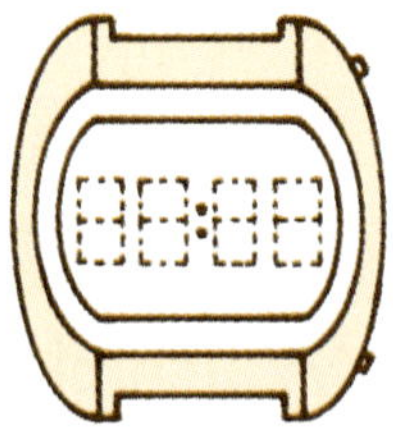

Grade

# ACTIVITY SHEET 18

**1.** Colour the hundred squares to show the decimals given.

a. 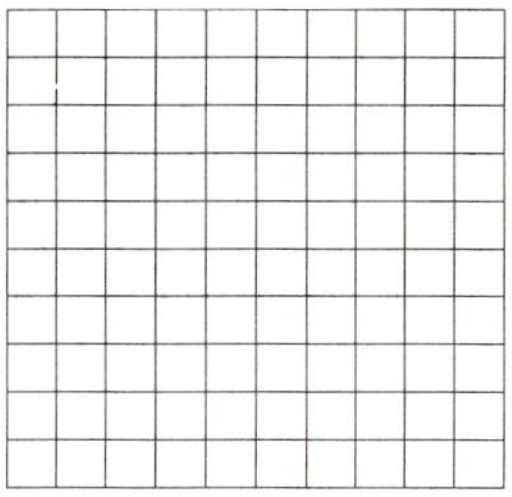 0.18

b. 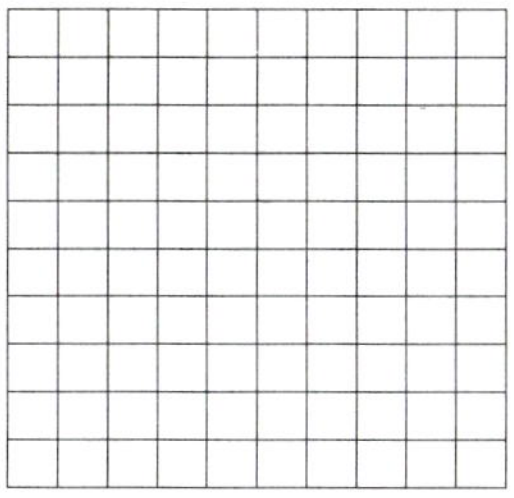 0.97

c. 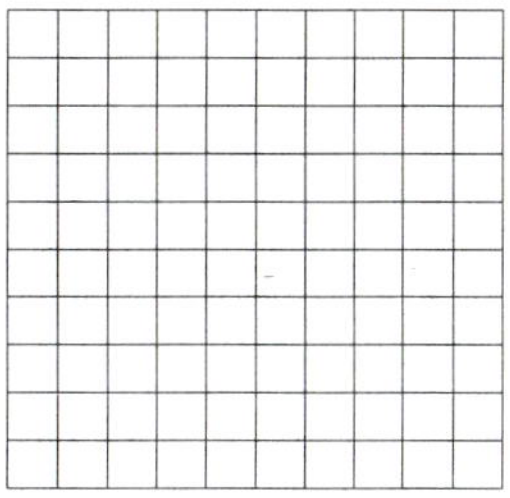 0.7

d. 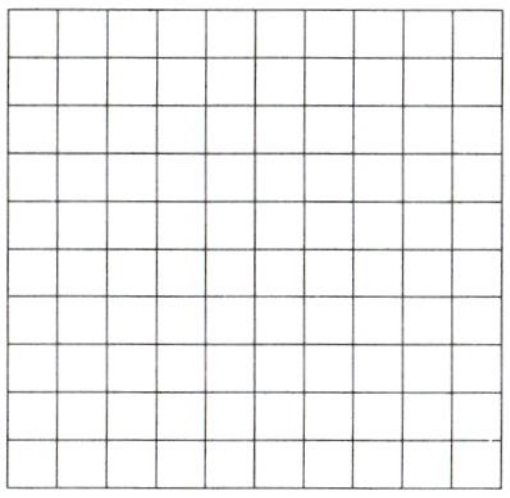 0.55

**2.** Complete the label for each hundred square.

a. 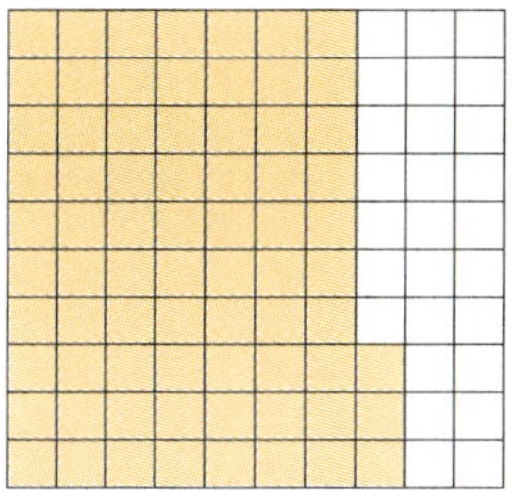

b. 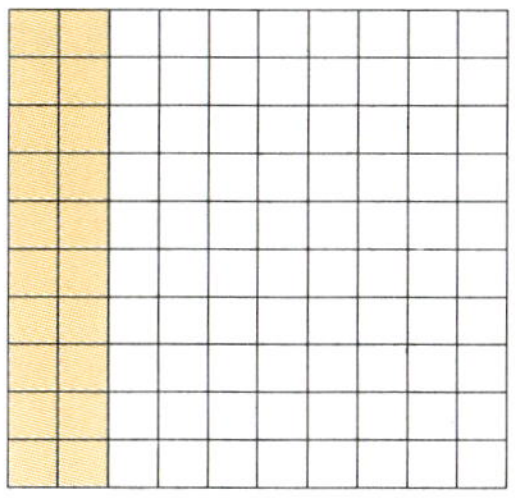

c. 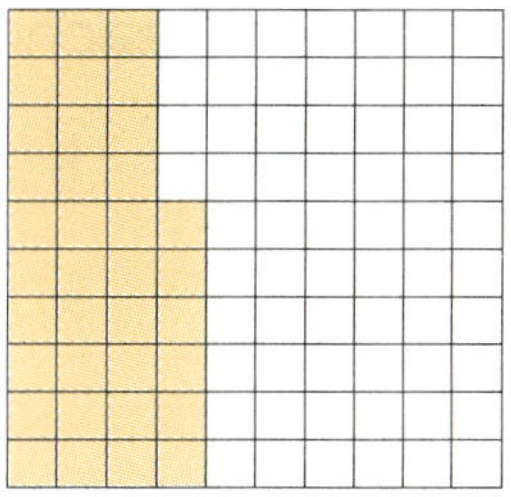

d. 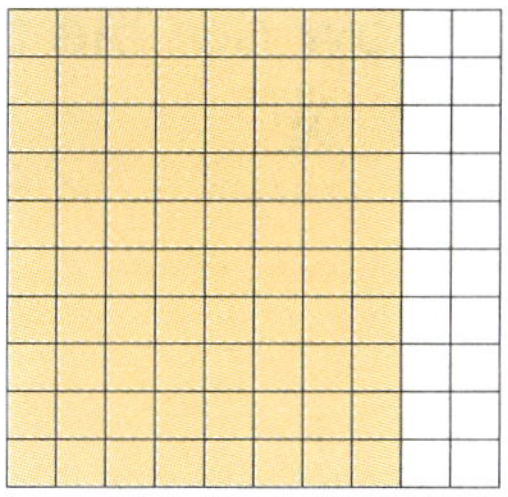

**3.** Look for the pattern and fill in the blanks.

a.

| | |
|---|---|
| 9 × 1 = 9 | 9 × 6 = ______ |
| 9 × 2 = 18 | 9 × 7 = ______ |
| 9 × 3 = 27 | 9 × 8 = ______ |
| 9 × 4 = 36 | 9 × 9 = ______ |
| 9 × 5 = 45 | 9 × 10 = ______ |

b.

| | |
|---|---|
| 19 × 1 = 19 | 19 × 6 = ______ |
| 19 × 2 = 38 | 19 × 7 = ______ |
| 19 × 3 = 57 | 19 × 8 = ______ |
| 19 × 4 = 76 | 19 × 9 = ______ |
| 19 × 5 = 95 | 19 × 10 = ______ |

# ACTIVITY SHEET 19

Grade

**1.** Measure these lines to the nearest centimetres.

a. ______________________________ = _____ cm

b. ______________________ = _____ cm

c. ___________________________ = _____ cm

d. _______________ = _____ cm

e. _________________________ = _____ cm

f. Which line(s) can be divided equally into two halves? _____

**2.** Now double the measure of each line and write the values.

a. _____ b. _____ c. _____

d. _____ e. _____

**3.** Draw all the axes of symmetry for each shape and count them to complete the table.

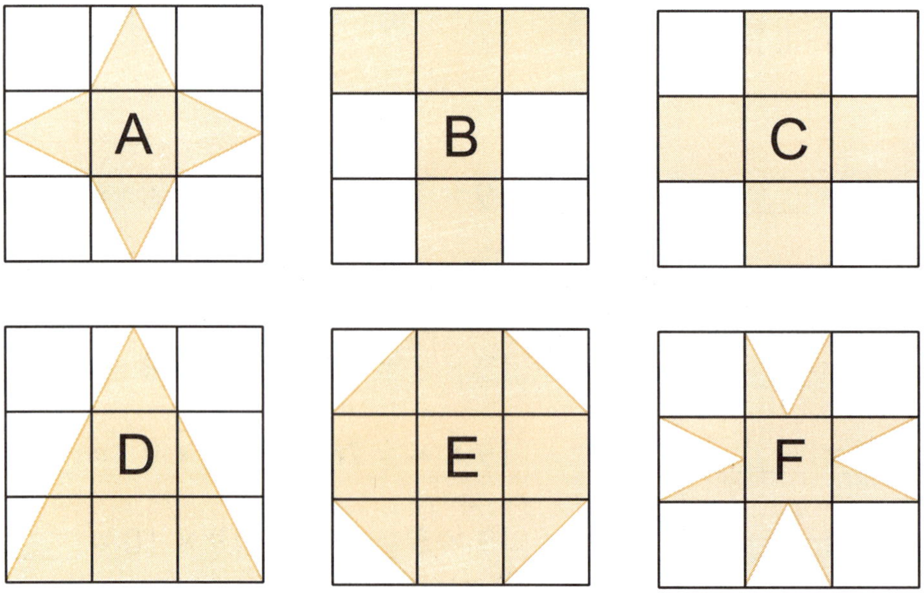

| | Number of Axes |
|---|---|
| A | |
| B | |
| C | |
| D | |
| E | |
| F | |

Grade

# ACTIVITY SHEET 20

**1.** Complete the copy for each isometric projection.

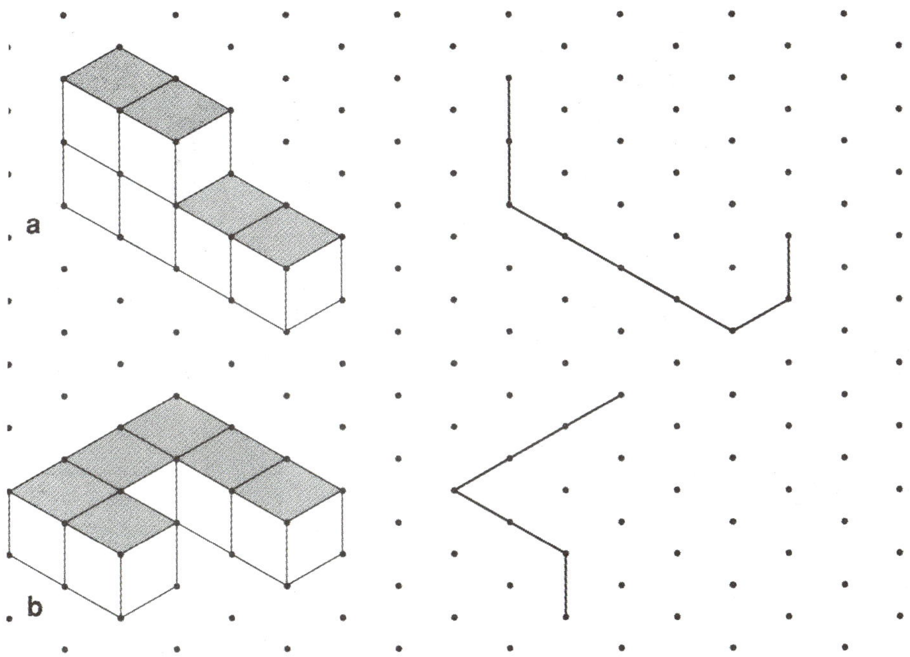


How many blocks are needed to build each model?

a. ______

b. ______

**2.** Complete the lunch orders. Find the total.

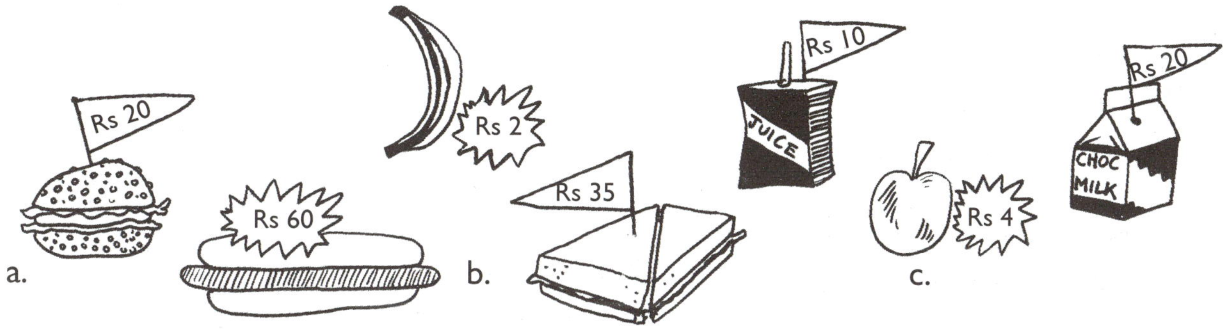


| Kamal | |
|---|---|
| 1 hot dog | ______ |
| 1 orange-juice | ______ |
| 2 bananas | ______ |
| Total | ______ |

| Geeta | |
|---|---|
| 1 sandwich | ______ |
| 1 choc milk | ______ |
| 2 apples | ______ |
| Total | ______ |

| Sangeeta | |
|---|---|
| 1 hamburger | ______ |
| 2 apples | ______ |
| 1 banana | ______ |
| 1 choc milk | ______ |
| Total | ______ |

# ACTIVITY SHEET 21

Grade

**1.** Priya followed the route on the map. Find the total distance she walked.

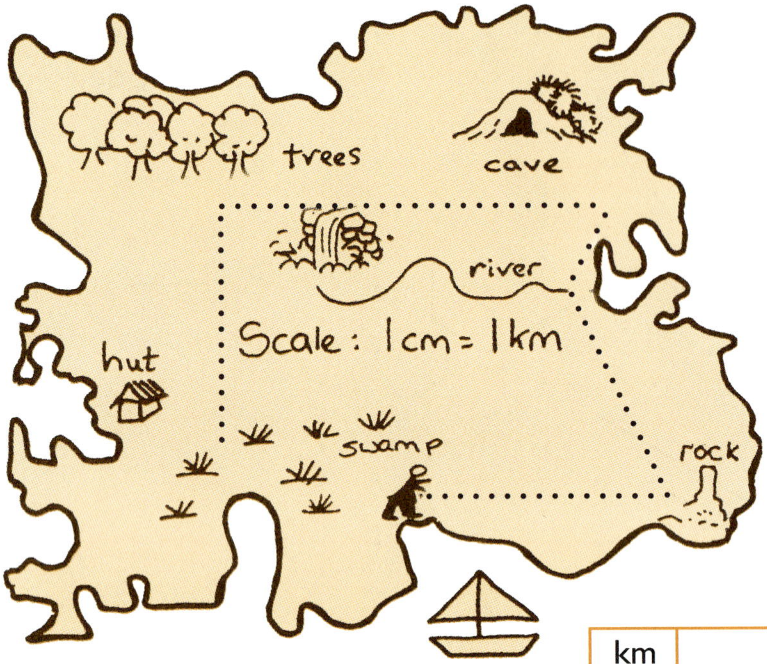

| km | + + + + = | | | | | |
|---|---|---|---|---|---|---|
| view | rock | river | cave | tree | hut | Total |

**2.** Use the given table to complete the sentences.

In this home

a. Which is the hottest place? _______

b. Which is the coolest place? _______

c. Which is cooler, the kitchen, or the family room? _______

d. Which is hotter, the bricked patio or grassy backyard? _______ By how much is it hotter? _______

e. What is the difference between the lowest and the highest temperature?

_______

| **Place** | **Temperature** |
|---|---|
| Kitchen | 34 °C |
| Family Room | 26 °C |
| Aluminium garden shed | 45 °C |
| Grassy backyard | 37 °C |
| Bricked patio | 40 °C |

Grade ☐

# ACTIVITY SHEET 22

**1.** Answer the following.

a. Which has a greater area, this page or your table top? ______

b. The unit used to measure a tank of petrol is ______

c. The unit used to measure a bag of onions is ______

d. The boiling point of water is ______

e. How many days in a leap year? ______

f. Rishu is 119 cm tall. Nishu is 127 cm tall. How much taller is Nishu? ______

g. Akshay played tennis for 3 hours. For how many minutes did he play? ______

h. The height of a power pole is about (55 cm; 1 m; 50 m). ______

i. Is 5019 greater than 5109? (yes/no). ______

j. What fraction of 1 kg is 200 g? ______

k. The date one week after 25th June is ______

**2.** a. What shape is located at

G5 ______

E5 ______

C2 ______

C1 ______

E1 ______

B3 ______

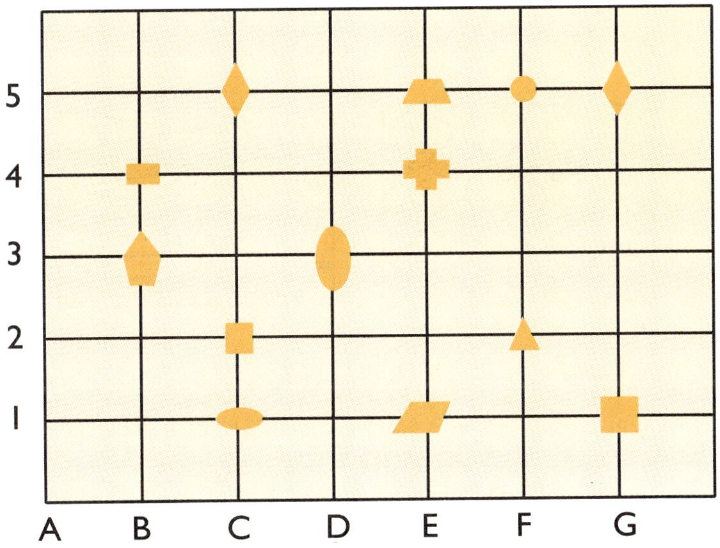


b. What are the coordinates of

 ______  ______  ______  ______

# ACTIVITY SHEET 23

Grade

**1.** Answer the following.

a. Minutes in 1.5 hours = ________

b. What fraction of 1 L is 500 mL? ________

c. Share Rs 180 equally among six children. How much will each get? ________

d. Rs 12.45 + Rs 1.25 = ________

e. 493 more than 5019 is _______

f. Does a kilogram of biscuits take the same space as a kilogram of rocks? ______

g. Does a kilogram of feathers fill the same space as a kilogram of sand? ______

h. The plane departed at 10.45 a.m. for a 2 hour flight.
Show the landing time on the given clock face.

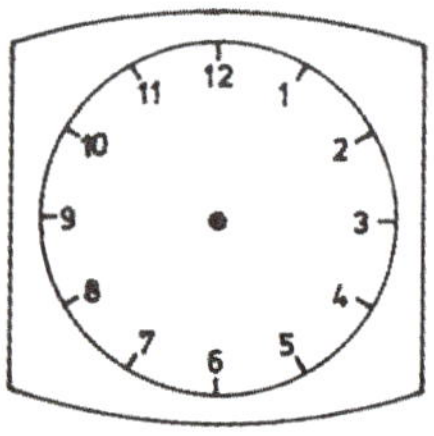


**2.** Colour the boxes which contain shapes that tessellate.

a.

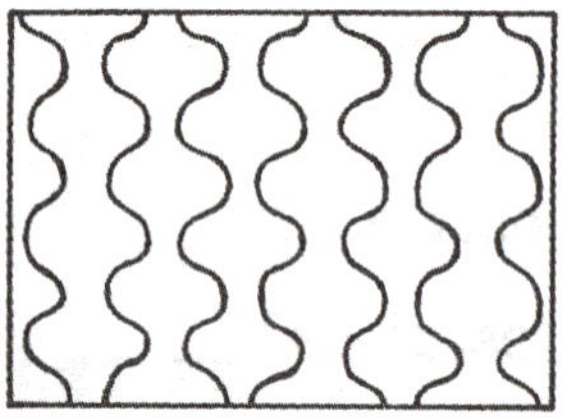

b.

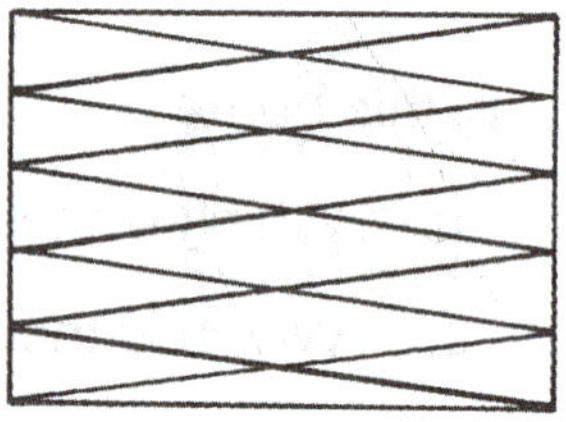

c.

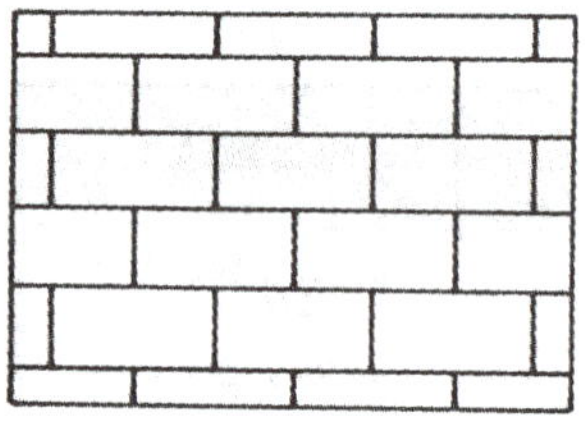

d.

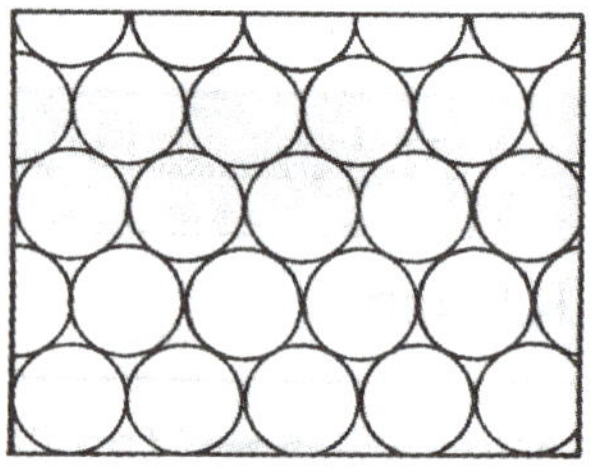

**3.** Colour the lines in the boxes as directed.

a. horizontal (red)

b. vertical (black)

c. diagonal (blue)

Grade

# ACTIVITY SHEET 24

**1.** Colour the two factors that multiply to give each central number.

a.
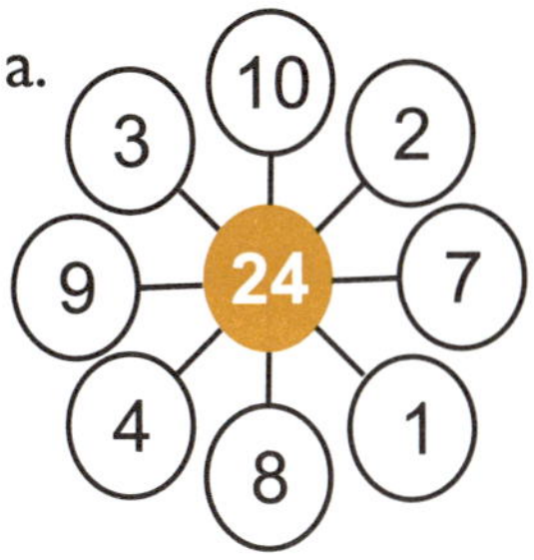


b.
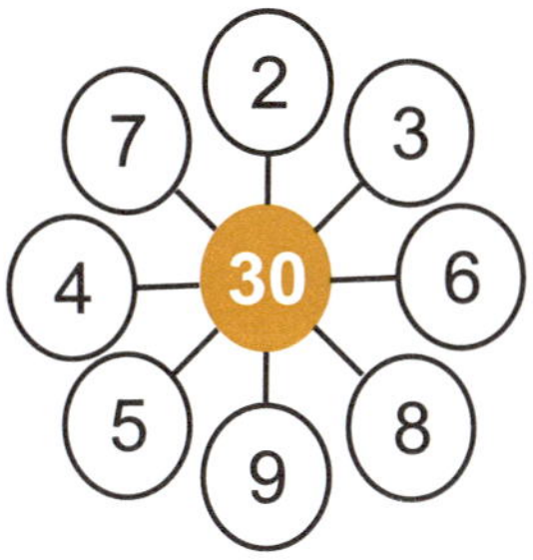


c.
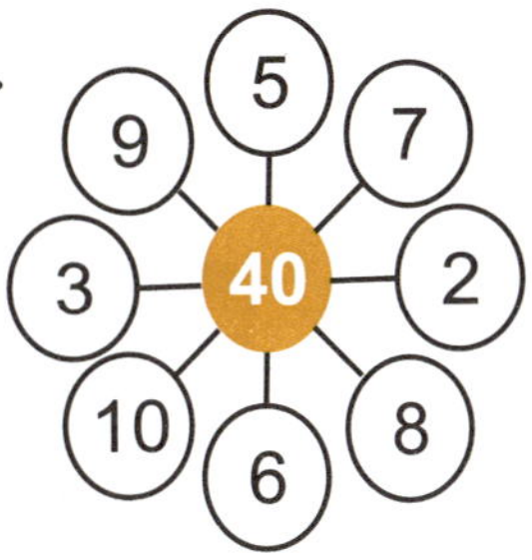


d.
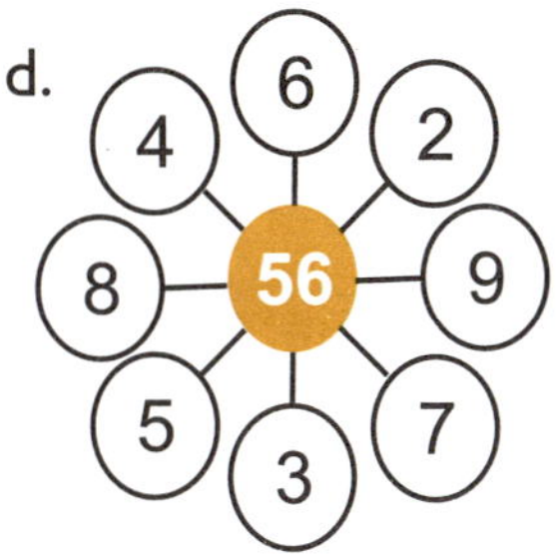


e.
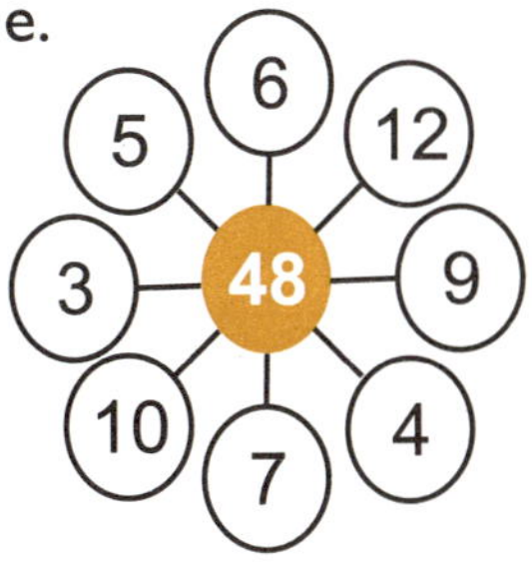


f.
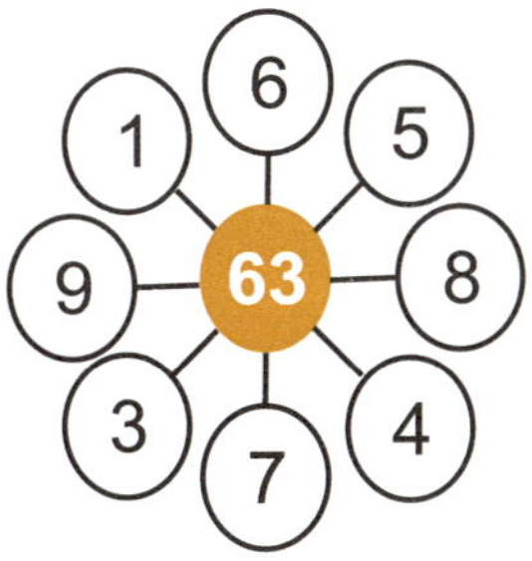


g.
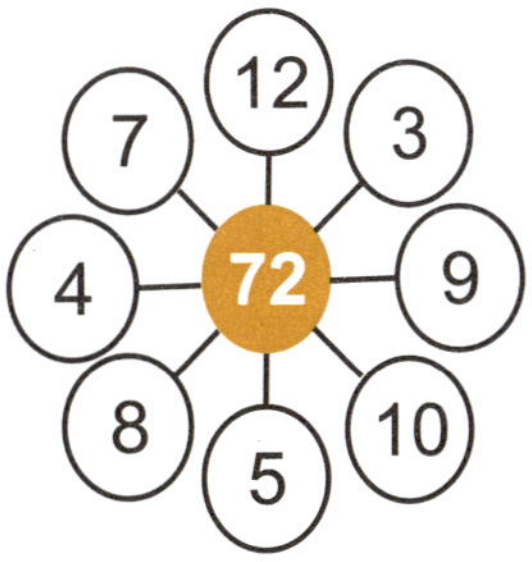


h.
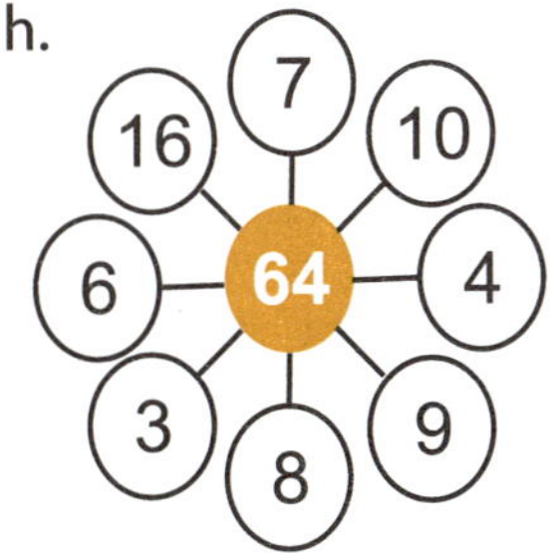


**2.** a. Write a 3-digit number which when divided by 15 gives 9. _______

b. Think of a number between 1 and 9. Multiply it by 2. Multiply the product by 4. Divide the product by 8. What do you get? ________________________

**3.** Calculate the number of cubes used to build each model.

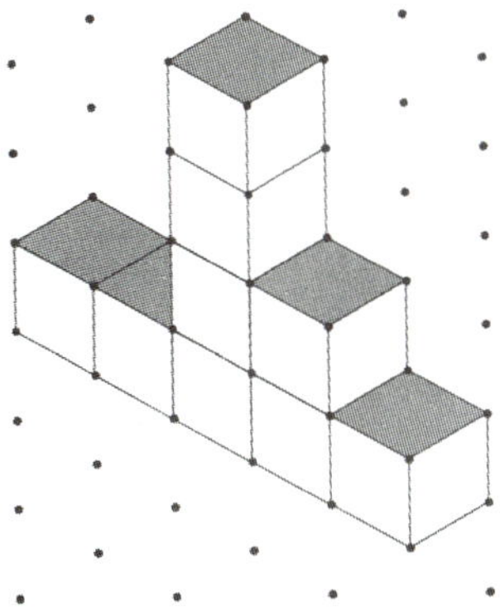

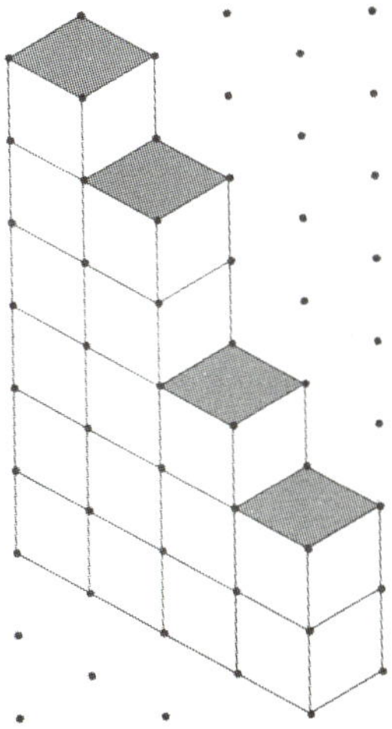

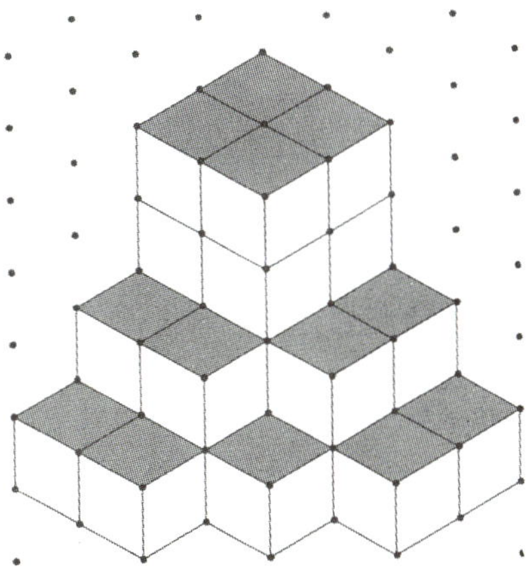

a. _______ cubes b. _______ cubes c. _______ cubes

# ACTIVITY SHEET 25

Grade

1. Complete each mirror image.

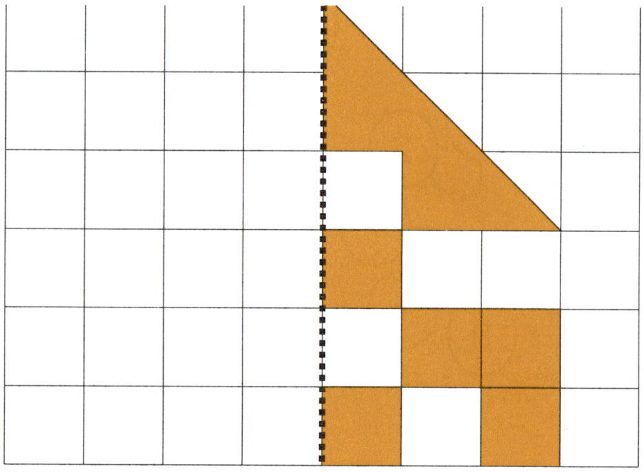

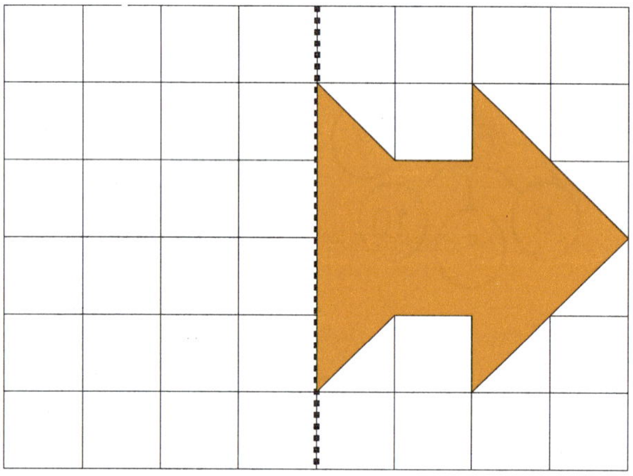

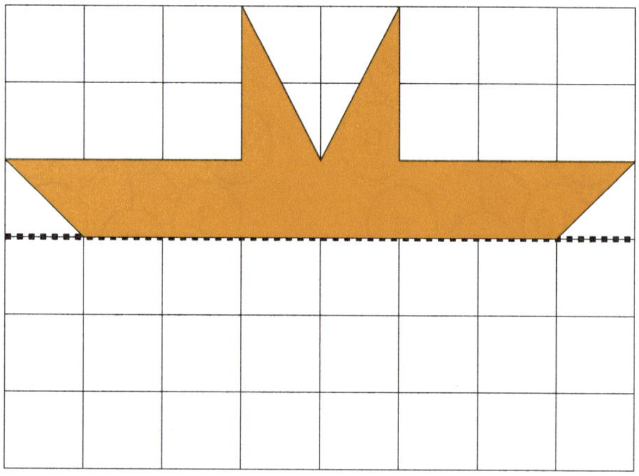

2. Look at the rates and answer the following.

a. What is the cost of 2 kg of cherries? ______

b. Can you buy 12 peaches in Rs 90? ______

c. The cost of 10 apples is ______

d. The cost of 1.5 dozen of bananas is ______

What is the total cost of

e. 1 pineapple and 2 dozens of bananas ______

f. 10 apples and 2 kg of cherries ______

g. 4 peaches and 2 pineapples ______

h. 4 apples and 1 dozen of bananas ______

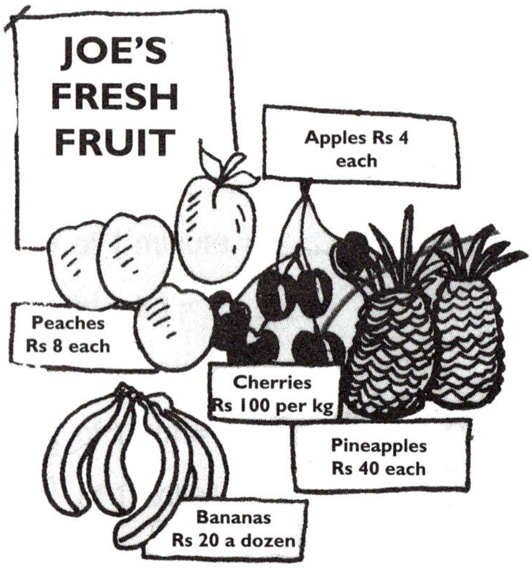

Grade

# ACTIVITY SHEET 26

**1.** What are the prime numbers between 10 and 20? ______________________

**2.** Shade part of each group to match the given fraction.

a.

$\frac{1}{4}$

b.

$\frac{3}{4}$

c.

$\frac{1}{2}$

d.

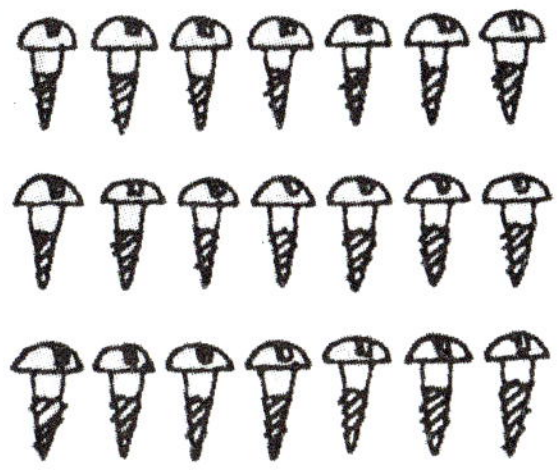

$\frac{5}{21}$

**3.** What fraction of each group is shaded?

a.

b.

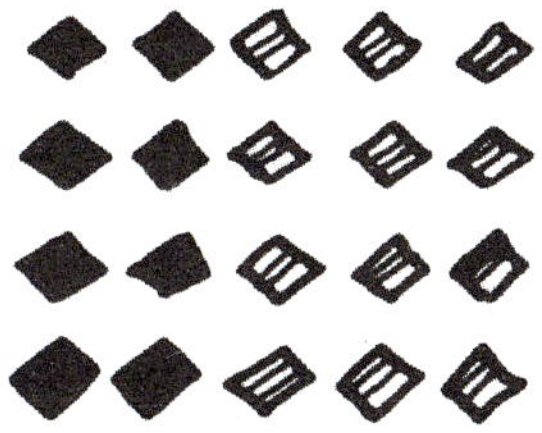

c.

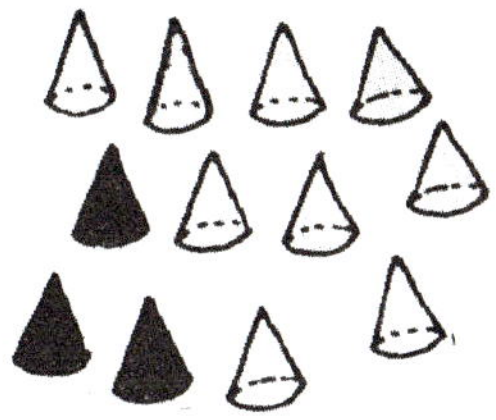

d.

**4.** Write a 4-digit number which when divided by 12 gives 90. ______

**5.** Write a 3-digit number which when divided by 16 gives 8. ______

**6.** Write the number that comes before the smallest 6-digit number. ______

**7.** Write the number that comes after the greatest 6-digit number. ______

# ACTIVITY SHEET 27

Grade

**1.** Answer the following.

a. $\frac{1}{2}$ of a year = ______ days

b. $\frac{1}{2}$ of ______ m = 50 cm

c. $\frac{1}{2}$ of 1 day = ______ hours

d. $\frac{1}{2}$ of 1 kg = ______ g

e. $\frac{1}{2}$ of a minute = ______ seconds

f. $\frac{1}{2}$ of 1 rupee = ______ paise

g. $\frac{1}{2}$ of 1 hour = ______ minutes

h. Centimetres in 1.96 m = ______

i. Write 20 past 2 in digital time. ______

j. Millilitres in 2.2 litres = ______

**2.** For each of the following patterns, find a simple rule and use it to write down the next five terms.

a. 1, 4, 7, 10, 13, ______, ______, ______, ______, ______,

b. 1, 4, 9, 16, 25, ______, ______, ______, ______, ______,

c. 1, 5, 10, 16, 23, ______, ______, ______, ______, ______,

d. 6, 11, 16, 21, 26, ______, ______, ______, ______, ______,

**3.** Use the least number of masses from the ones given below to nearly balance each scale.

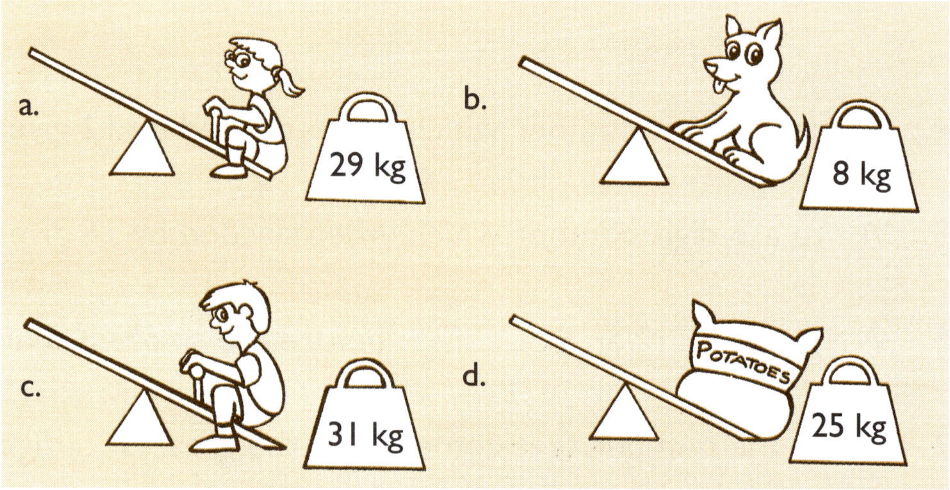

Grade

# ACTIVITY SHEET 28

**Make a seven-piece tangram.**

1. Use any sized square of paper or a thin board.

2. Fold both diagonals.

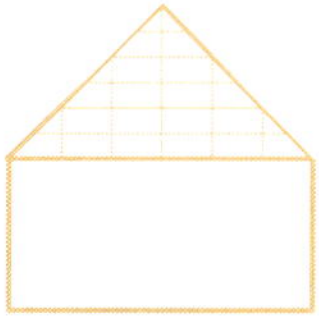

3. Fold the 2 upper corners to the centre.

4. Fold out flat. Fold the left hand edge to the centre.

5. Fold out flat. Rule the fold lines as shown. Label each shape and carefully cut into the seven pieces.

Folded  Ruled 

**1.** Compare the seven pieces. Notice some similarities.

a. What is the relationship between G and F? ______

b. What plane shape is D? ______

c. Is the area of A equal to the area of C + E? ______

d. How many triangles do you have? ______

e. What is common to all the triangles? ______________________________

f. What plane shapes can be made if we join G and F? ____________________

g. What plane shapes can be made if we join E, B and C? _________________

# ACTIVITY SHEET 29

Grade

Use your tangram made in the previous activity to make these pictures.

1. Arrange your pieces to re-form the original square.

2. Make another square using F and G.
3. Which other 2 triangles will form a square? ______________
4. Use pieces B, C, and E to make these shapes and label the shapes below.

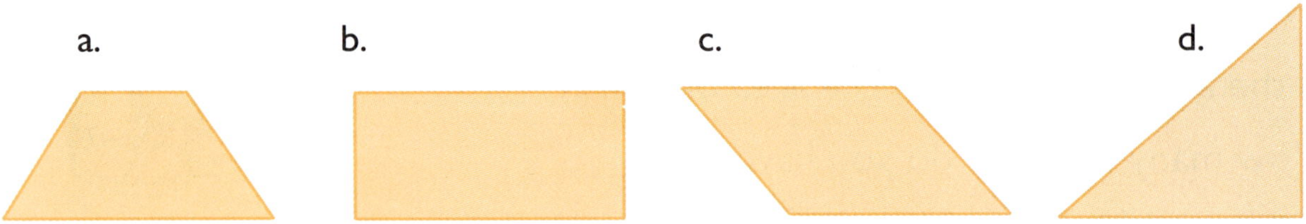


______________ ______________ ______________ ______________

Show the outlines of the 3 pieces on each shape above.

Grade

# ACTIVITY SHEET 30

**1.** Fill in the blanks.

a. The number 106 before 4064 is ______

b. One hundred ana two X thirty-six = ______

c. 3000 + 400 + 20 + 6 = ______

d. (6 × 100) + (4 × 10) + 7 = ______

e. Two hundred and ninety-five ÷ 10 = ______

f. 6000 + 30 + 8 = ______

g. ______ = 400 + 50 + 7

h. 8 days after 25th June ______

i. ______ = 5000 ÷ 50

j. 11 days after 25th December ______

k. (5 × 1000) + (3 × 100) + (2 × 10) + 4 = ______

l. 20000 + 6000 + 400 + 30 + 7 = ______

**2.** Arrange in ascending order:

a. 2319, 2139, 239, 2193 ______________________

b. 5087, 5870, 5780, 5807 ______________________

**3.** What fraction of each has been shaded?

a.

b.

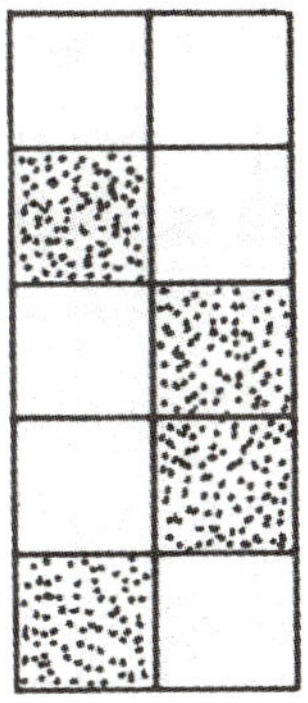

c.

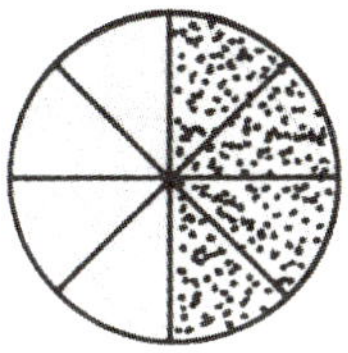

d.

e.

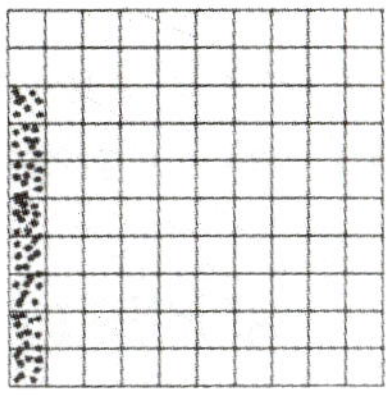

f.

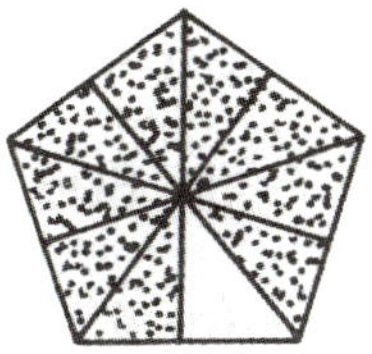

# ACTIVITY SHEET 31

Grade

**1.** Use the coordinates below to plot a course on the grid.

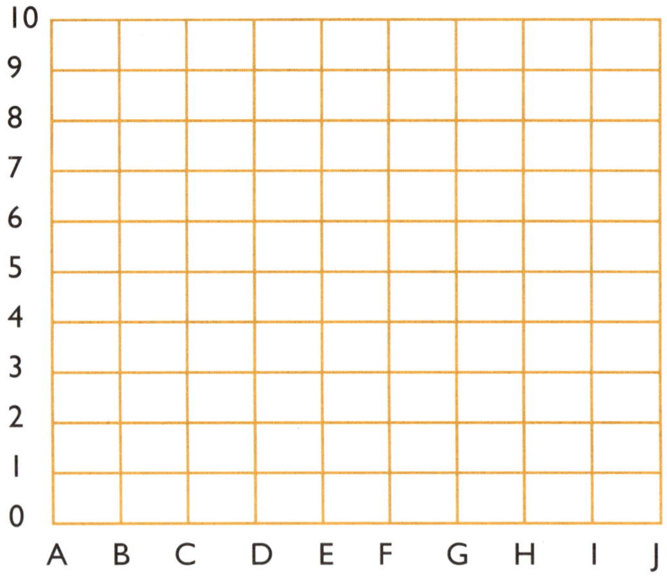


B10, B4, H4, B2, B0, J0, J6, D6, D8, J8, J10, B10

Join the dots to show the letter.

________

**2.** What unit of measure would you use for

a. the water in an overhead tank ______

b. the mass of an egg ______

c. the height of a giraffe ______

d. the area of a small room ______

e. the volume of a shoe-box ______

f. the medicine in a bottle ______

g. the length of your arm ______

h. the mass of a bag of rice ______

i. the length of your recess break ______

j. the area of your classroom ______

k. the length of your trousers ______

l. the distance from Mumbai to Goa ______

m. the length of time at school in one day ______

**3.** Show 20 minutes after 6:50.

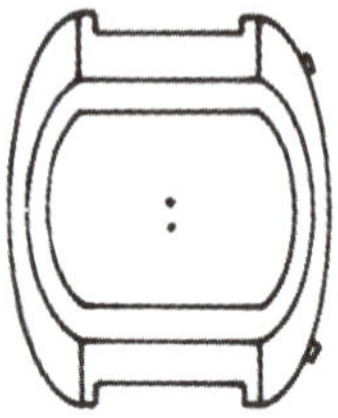


**4.** Show 15 minutes before 3:10.

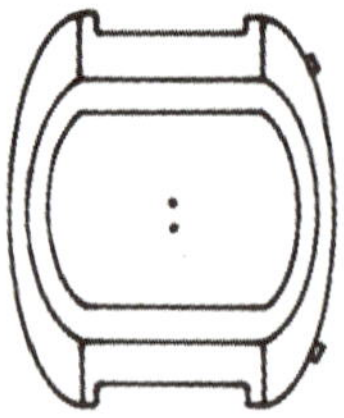

Grade

# ACTIVITY SHEET 32

**1.** Read the TV guide and answer the following.

a. How long in minutes is the programme:

Sunday Disney ______

Movie ______

Krishna ______

Smash Hits ______

b. What programme follows:

Quiz Show ______

Real Life ______

c. How long is it between the end of The Noon News and the start of News Sport and Weather? ______

| | |
|---|---|
| 9:30 | Sunday Disney - For Kids |
| 11:00 | Smash Hits |
| 12:00 | The Noon News |
| 12:30 | Movie : Rang de Basanti |
| 3:00 | My Three Sons |
| 4:00 | Fox kids |
| 4:30 | Afternoon Show - For Kids |
| 5:30 | Quiz Show |
| 6:00 | News, Sport and Weather |
| 6:30 | Real Life - Current Affairs |
| 7:00 | Krishna |
| 8:00 | KBC 2 |

**2.** Double the area of these triangles to form quadrilaterals. Calculate the area of each quadrilateral. Assume each square to be of 1 cm side.

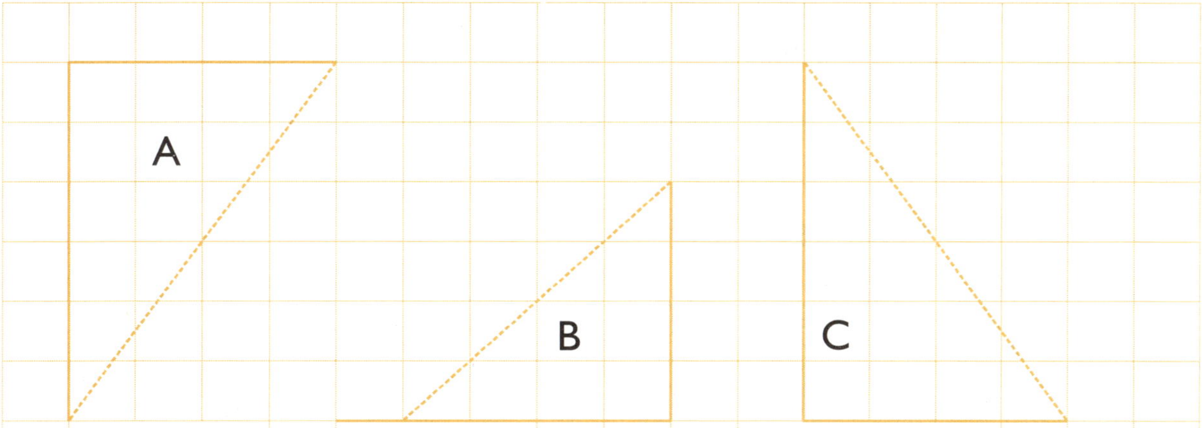


Area ______ Area ______ Area ______

# ACTIVITY SHEET 33

Grade

Study the graph, and answer the following.

**Sale of Sunscreen**

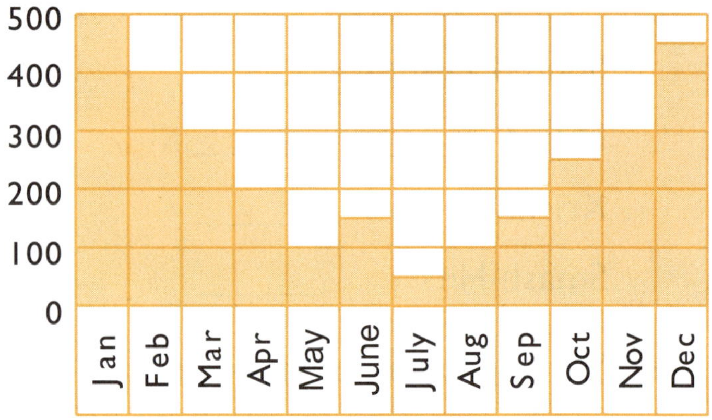


**1.** Which month had

a. most sales ______

b. least sales ______

c. 250 sales ______

d. 400 sales ______

**2.** Which months had

a. more than 300 sales ______________

b. less than 150 sales ______________

c. 300 sales______________

**3.** How many sales were made in winters? ______

**4.** Answer the following.

a. The number halfway between 1920 and 1980 is ______

b. Hindu Arabic numeral for XLIII is ______

c. The normal human heart beats 72 times a minute. What are the number of heartbeats in four hours? ______

d. Which is larger $8^2$ or $9 \times 7$? ______

e. Every month a child gains about 300 g of weight. How much weight would be gained in 2 years? ______

f. What number follows 63599? ______

g. John's mother was born 28 years before John. If John is 13 years old now, how old is his mother? ______

**5.** Which unit of measure ($cm^2$ or $m^2$) would you use to find the area of

a. your seat ______

b. the floor of your classroon ______

c. this page ______

d. the wall of your classroom ______

Time: 15 minutes

Score ________

# 2 Quiz - Time

**1.** What number is 80 less than 5708? ________

**2.** 8000 less 3000 equals, 2000 more than ________

**3.** Mohan had Rs 1000. He spent Rs 650. The money left with him is ________

**4.** There are 85 passengers travelling on a bus. Twenty passengers get off and 18 get on. How many passengers are there in the bus now? ________

**5.** If half a number is 152 less than 200, what is the number? ________

**6.** Write the number of days from 28th July to 12th August. ________

**7.** If today's date is 16th December, then what will be the date after 23 days.

________

**8.** How many wheels are there in 3000 tricycles? ________

**9.** Write at least 6 problems so that the answer is 10, 000. One has been done for you.

a. 20, 000 ÷ 2 = 10, 000 or 9, 500 + 500 = 10, 000

b. ________

c. ________

d. ________

e. ________

f. ________

g. ________

# ACTIVITY SHEET 34

Grade ☐

Class 4 counted vehicles outside their school gate and prepared this graph. Read it and answer the following questions.

**1.** What type of vehicle was seen

a. most often ______

b. least often ______

c. 48 times ______

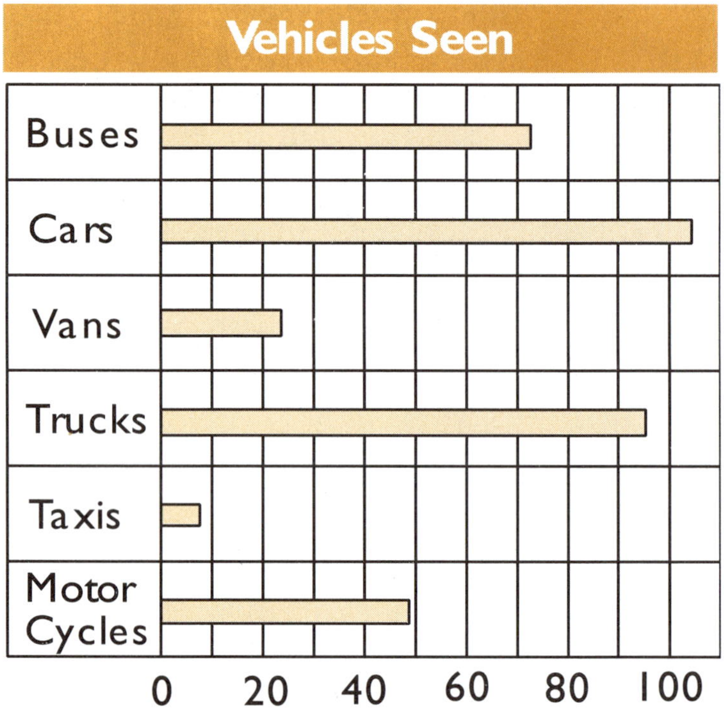


**2.** Were motor cycles seen

a. more often than the vans but less than cars ______

b. less often than trucks but more than buses ______

**3.** Round off to the nearest ten, the number of

a. buses ______

b. cars ______

**4.** For each object, write the name of the solid shape it resembles most.

a.  ______

b. 

______

c.  ______

d. 

______

e.  ______

f.  ______

g.  ______

h. 

______

# ACTIVITY SHEET 35

**1.** Calculate the number of cubes used to build each model.

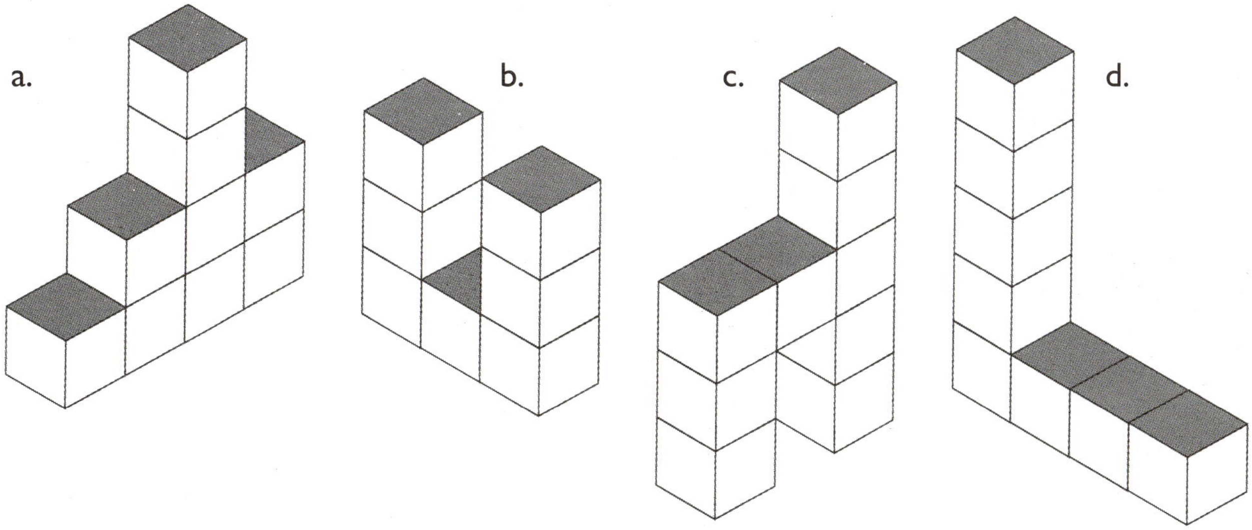


a. _______ cubes b. _______ cubes c. _______ cubes d. _______ cubes

**2.** If the volume of each small cube is 1 $cm^3$, find the volume of each model.

a. _______ b. _______ c. _______ d. _______

**3.** Model and draw some pentacubes of your own.

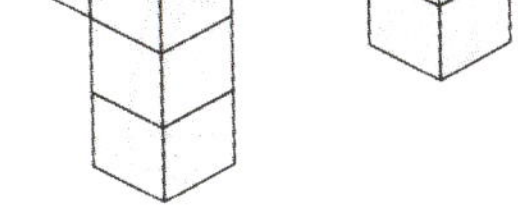

*Pentacubes use 5 cubes.*

# ACTIVITY SHEET 36

Grade

**1.** Complete the table for these shapes. Assume each small square to be of 6 cm side.

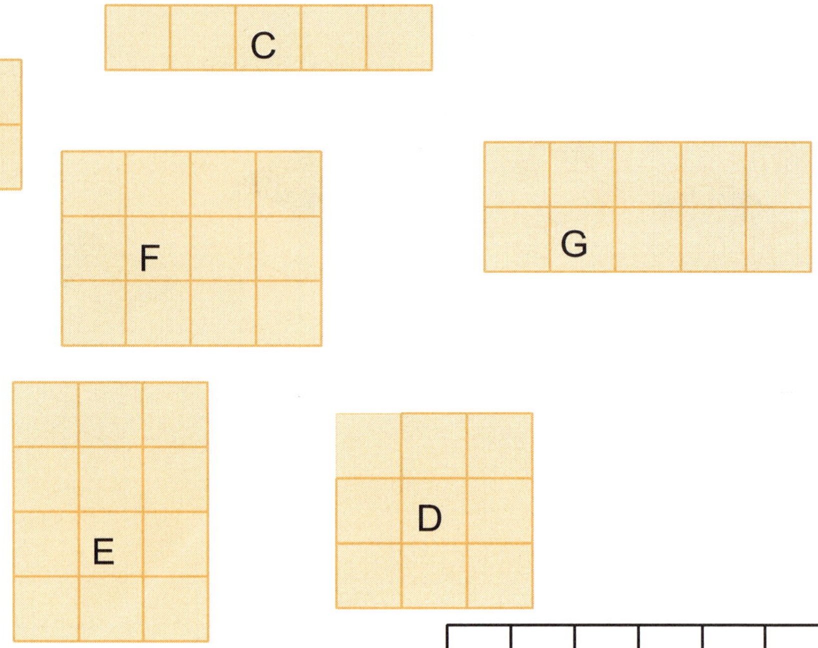


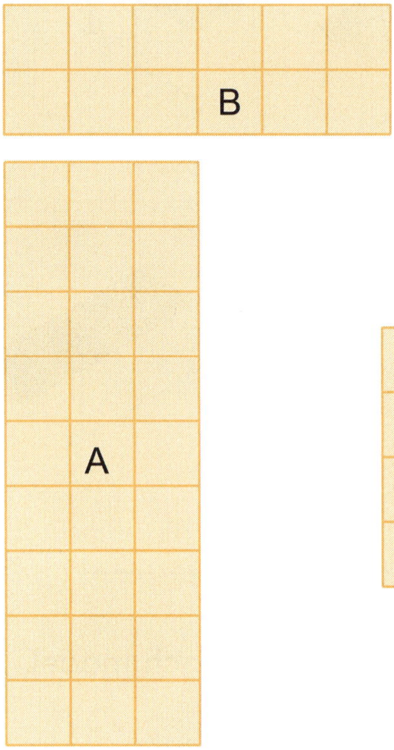


| | A | B | C | D | E | F | G |
|---|---|---|---|---|---|---|---|
| Perimeter (cm) | | | | | | | |
| Area ($cm^2$) | | | | | | | |

**2.** Add the correct unit of measure. ($cm^3$ or $m^3$)

a. 12000 ______

b. 4 ______

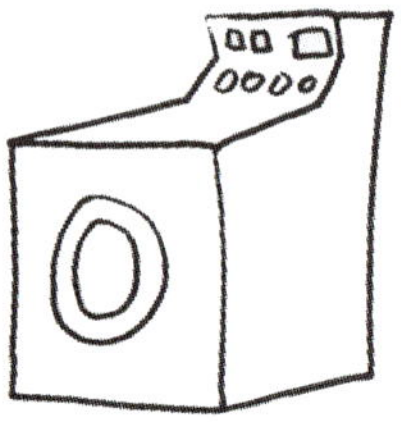

c. 1 ______

d. 800 ______

e. 40 ______

f. 4000 ______

Grade

# ACTIVITY SHEET 37

**1.** On these thermometers show the approximate temperature of

a. b. c. d. e.

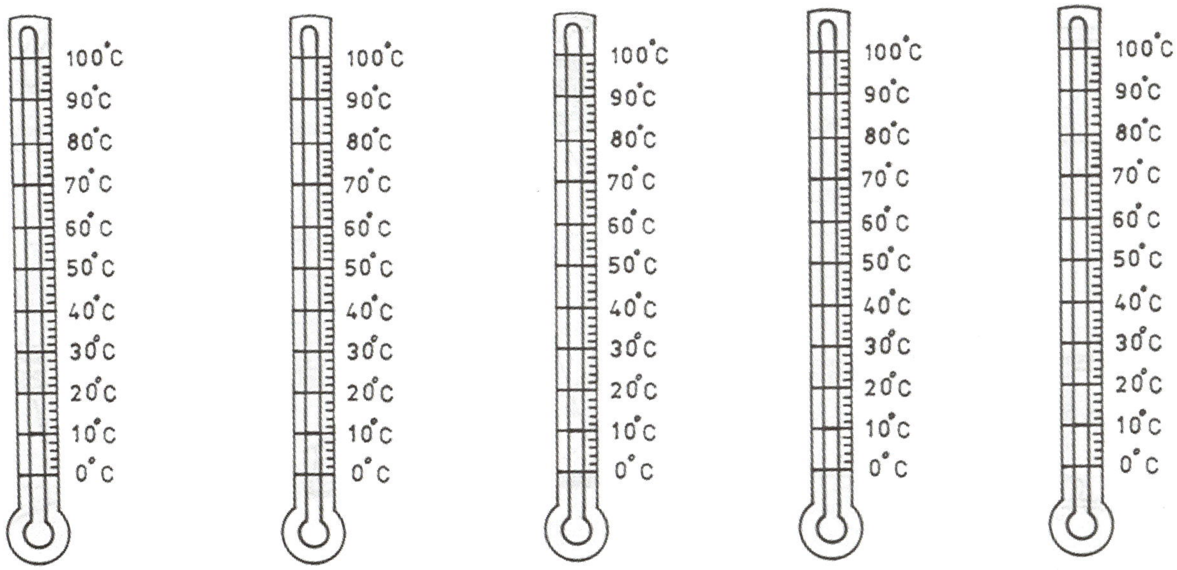


| a. | b. | c. | d. | e. |
|---|---|---|---|---|
| freshly boiled soup | normal human body temperature | refrigerated food | rain water | iced water |

**2.** Which of these plane shapes are

a. hexagons ______

b. quadrilaterals ______

c. triangles ______

d. pentagons ______

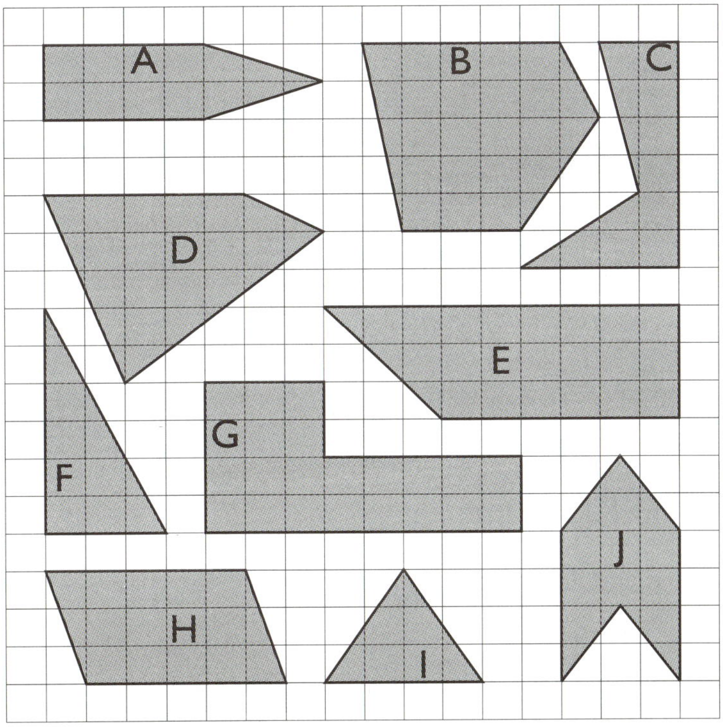

# ACTIVITY SHEET 38

Grade

**1.** Answer the following.

a. Which is smaller $10^2$ or 97? ______

b. Write three-fifths as a fraction. ______

c. Write 53 as Roman Numeral. ______

d. Roman Numeral of 69 ______

e. One-tenth of 40 ______

f. Increase 4967 by 100 ______

g. Place value of 7 in 27519 is ______

h. One-eighth of 160 ______

i. 60000 + 1000 + 900 + 30 + 5 = ______

j. (2 x 15) + (5 x 4) = ______

k. Difference between 286 and 350 ______

l. Round off 8525 to the nearest thousand. ______

m. Are 16 and 46 multiples of 6 (yes/no). ______

n. Write 46107 in words. ______________________________

Saurabh measured the weights of different number of eggs and graphed his findings. He then joined the points to get this line graph.

**2.** What is the weight of

a. 1 egg ______

b. 3 eggs ______

c. 5 eggs ______

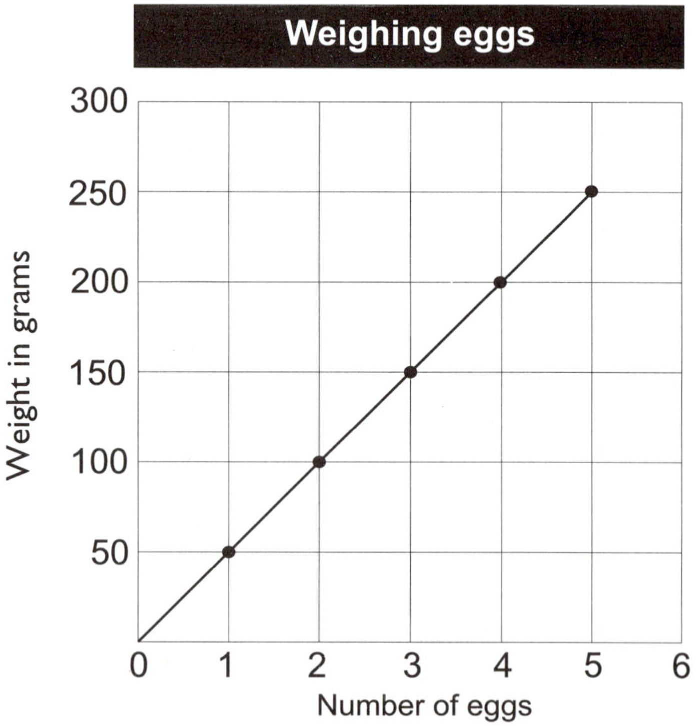


**3.** How many eggs have a total mass of

a. 50 grams ______

b. 100 grams ______

c. 200 grams ______

**4.** What would be the total weight of 6 eggs? ______

Grade

# ACTIVITY SHEET 39

**1.** From the given figure, calculate these distances in metres:

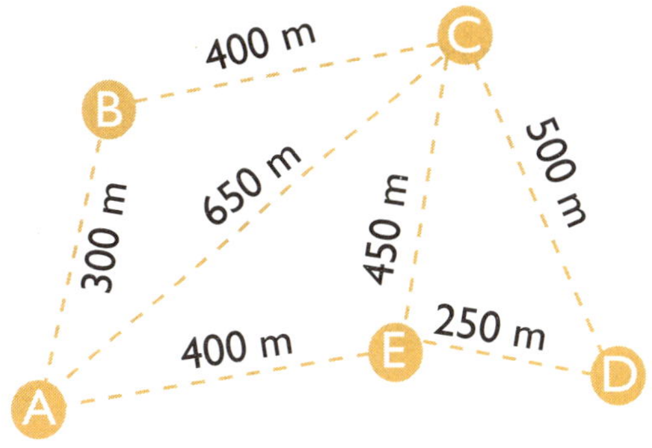


a. From C, through B to A ______

b. From A, through E to D ______

c. From C, through E and A to B ______

d. From B, through C and E to A ______

e. From A, through E, D and C to B ______

Round the Island Treasure Hunt

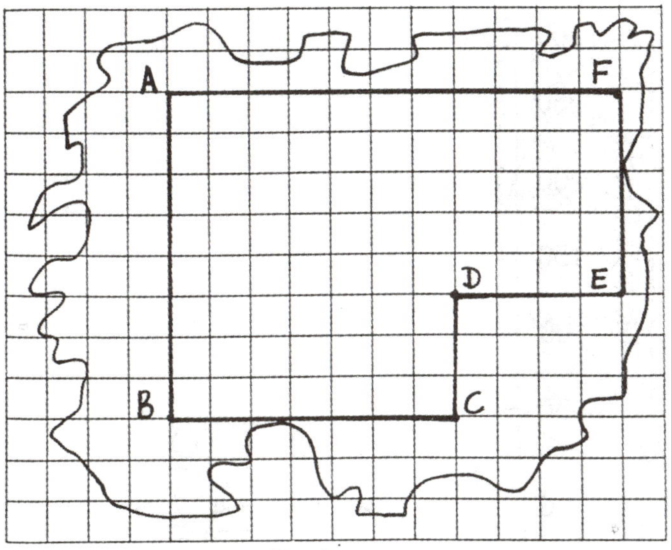


Scale

m 0 50 100 150 200 250

**2.** Find the distance travelled between

a. A and B ______ m

b. B and C ______ m

c. C and D ______ m

d. D and E ______ m

e. E and F ______ m

f. F and A ______ m

**3.** Find the total distance travelled. ______ m

**4.** Estimate the following:

a. The distance between your school and home ______

b. Distance from Delhi to Agra ______

c. Distance between your home and the Railway Station ______

d. Distance between your class-room and the main gate of the school ______

# ACTIVITY SHEET 40

Grade

**1.** Write the numbers in figures.

a. Three hundred forty-four thousand nine hundred and sixteen ____________

b. Sixty-one lakhs fourteen thousand two hundred and thirty-five ____________

c. Eight crores three lakhs fourty-six thousand and fifty-one ____________

d. Two million two hundred forty thousand seven hundred and seventy-two ____________

**2.** Look at the figure shown below. Write true or false for the following statements.

a. AO = OD ________

b. CD = EF ________

c. OB = CH ________

d. CD = 2 × AO ________

e. EAOC is a square. ________

f. E, F, G and H are points. ________

g. AB is the diameter of the circle only. ________

h. AO is the radius of the circle. ________

i. O is the centre of both the circle and the square. ________

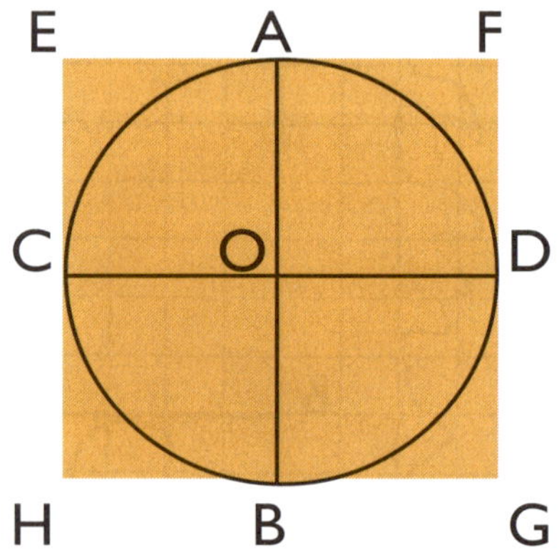


**3.** Write the numbers in expanded form.

a. 9,60,373 ______________________________

b. 8,48,531 ______________________________

c. 4,00,000 ______________________________

d. 2,00,012 ______________________________

Grade

# ACTIVITY SHEET 41

**1.** Measure the length of each side and find the perimeter of both the shapes.

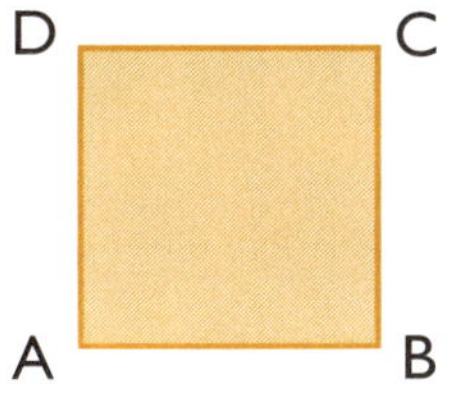

a. ____________ b. ____________

Now draw in the diagonals for each of the above shape and complete:

c. The sides of the square are

______________________________

d. The diagonals of the square are

______________________________

e. The sides of the rectangle are

______________________________

f. The diagonals of the rectangle are

______________________________

**2.** Mayank had Rs 250 to spend. He can buy 3 milkshakes and

a. 6 burgers

b. 5 burgers

c. 3 burgers

**3.** Joe bought ten exercise books. How much did he pay altogether? ________

**4.** Sam wanted to buy some rice.

Which bag gives better value for money?

a. 1.5 kg

b. 5 kg

**5.** Tony wanted to buy a shirt and a pair of shorts. He could buy with

a. Ten 20-rupee notes

b. Five 50-rupee notes

c. Five 100-rupee notes

# ACTIVITY SHEET 42

Grade

**1.** Answer the following.

a. Which is greatest: $7^2$; $4^2+3^2$; $50-2$; $40+7$

b. Write the Roman Numeral for 570. ______

c. The number halfway between 50,000 and 60,000. ______

d. Name the regular polygon that has 5 equal sides. ______

e. If the wall of a room is made of 200 bricks, estimate the total number of bricks used to make a cubic room. ______

f. Do the bricks on a wall tessellate? ______

g. How many sides has a hexagon? ______

h. What is the perimeter of a regular hexagonal table of side 2 metres? ______

i. How many corners has an octagon? ______

j. What is the total number of sides in 11 octagons? ______

k. Write two like fractions with the denominator 10. ______

l. A man walks 5 km daily except Sundays. Estimate the distance he will walk in two months. ______

m. Write 12963 in words ______________________________

**2.** Complete the following table.

| | | | | |
|---|---|---|---|---|
| 50 hundredths | 50 / 100 | 0.50 | 0.5 | 5 / 10 |
| | | | 0.8 | |
| | | 0.20 | | |
| | 30 / 100 | | | |
| | | 0.70 | | 7 / 10 |
| 10 hundredths | | | | |
| | | | 0.4 | 4 / 10 |
| | 100 / 100 | | | |

Grade

# ACTIVITY SHEET 43

**1.** Use DMRC time table to find the time taken to go from:

| | |
|---|---|
| Pragati Maidan | 11:50 a.m. |
| Barakhamba Road | 11:54 a.m. |
| Rajiv Chowk | 11:57 a.m. |
| Rama Krishna Ashram | 12:02 p.m. |
| Karol Bagh | 12:06 p.m. |
| Rajendra Place | 12:10 p.m. |
| Patel Nagar | 12:17 p.m. |
| Kirti Nagar | 12:22 p.m. |
| Moti Nagar | 12:27 p.m. |
| Ramesh Nagar | 12:32 p.m. |
| Tagore Garden | 12:35 p.m. |

a. Pragati Maidan to Rajiv Chowk ______

b. Rama Krishna Ashram to Moti Nagar ______

c. Barakhamba Road to Rajendra Place ______

d. Pragati Maidan to Tagore Garden ______

**2.** If the next train is half an hour later, when will it arrive at:

a. Pragati Maidan ______

b. Tagore Garden ______

**3.** If the train is 10 minutes early when will it arrive at:

a. Patel Nagar ______

b. Karol Bagh ______

**4.** Study the table and answer the following:

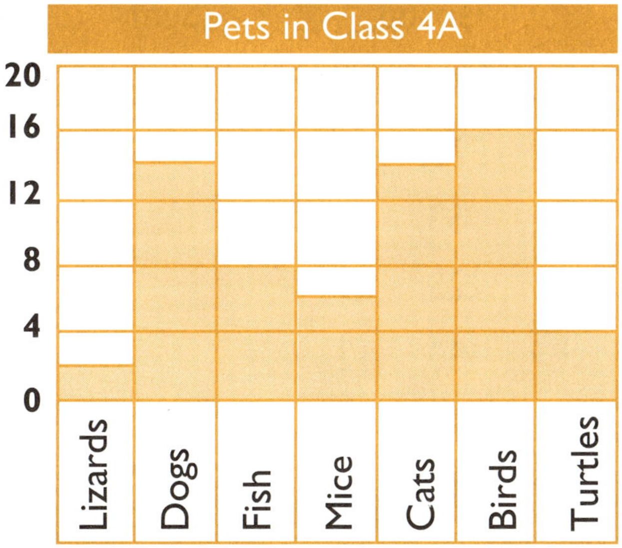


a. Which was the most popular pet? ______

b. Which was the least popular pet? ______

c. Which pets were equally popular? ______

d. How many pets were birds? ______

e. How many pets were fish? ______

f. What was the total number of cats, dogs, and birds? ______

# ACTIVITY SHEET 44

Grade

1. Find the perimeter of each shape.

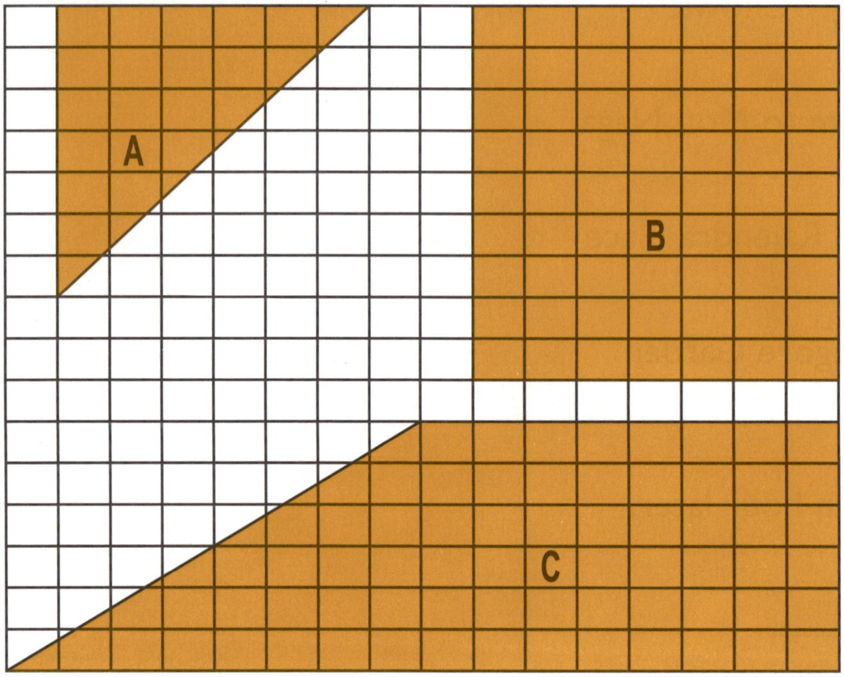


Scale: ▭ = 1 cm

a. A ______

b. B ______

c. C ______

2. Calculate the algorithms for each group of numbers.

| Group | Sum | Product | Difference | Quotient |
|---|---|---|---|---|
| 1600, 16 | | | | |
| 576, 24 | | | | |
| 53, 7 | | | | |
| 225, 25 | | | | |
| 480, 12 | | | | |
| 510, 17 | | | | |
| 1300, 26 | | | | |

Grade

# ACTIVITY SHEET 45

**1.** Plotting patterns

Plot each set of points.
Join each one to the next.

a. B1, B7, H7, H1, B1

b. B3, B5, D7, F7, H5, H3, F1, D1, B3

c. B4, E7, H4, E1, B4

d. D4, E6, H4, E2, D4

e. Colour the pattern you have made.

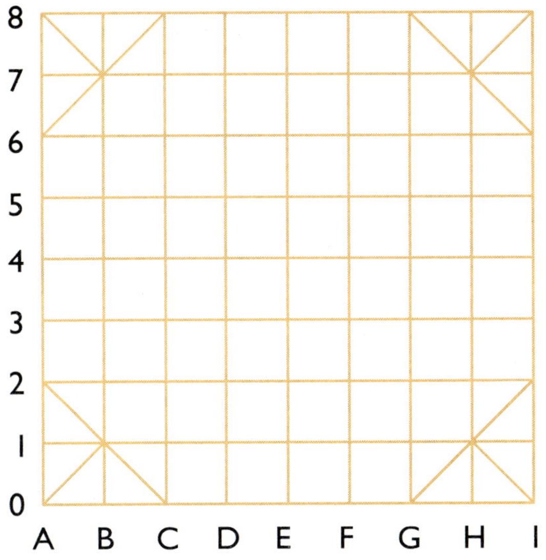


**2.** How many triangles of any size can you see in each?

a.

______

b.

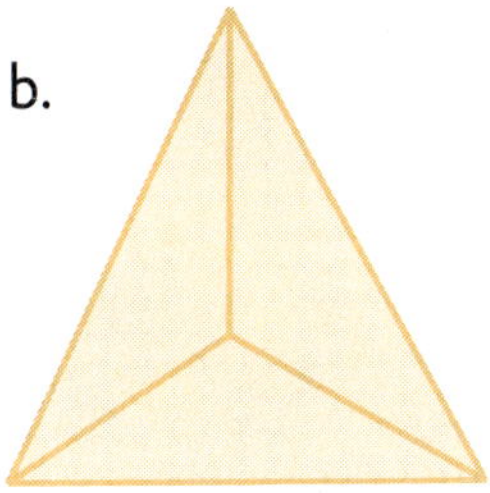

______

c.

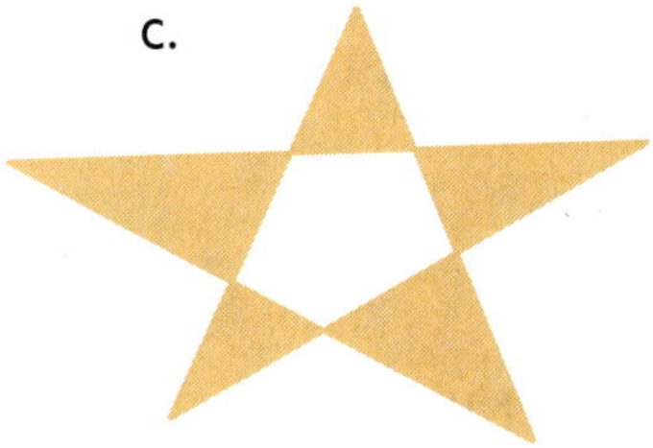

______

**3.** How many squares of any size can you see in each?

a.

______

b.

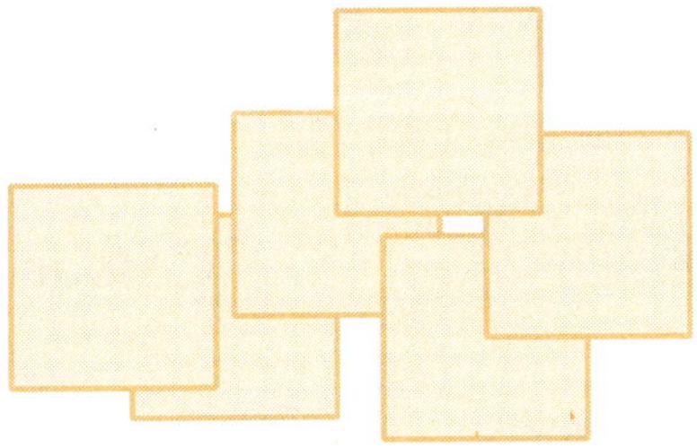

______

c.

______

# ACTIVITY SHEET 46

Grade

**1.** Complete these tessellating hexagons and rule more. Pattern or colour your design.

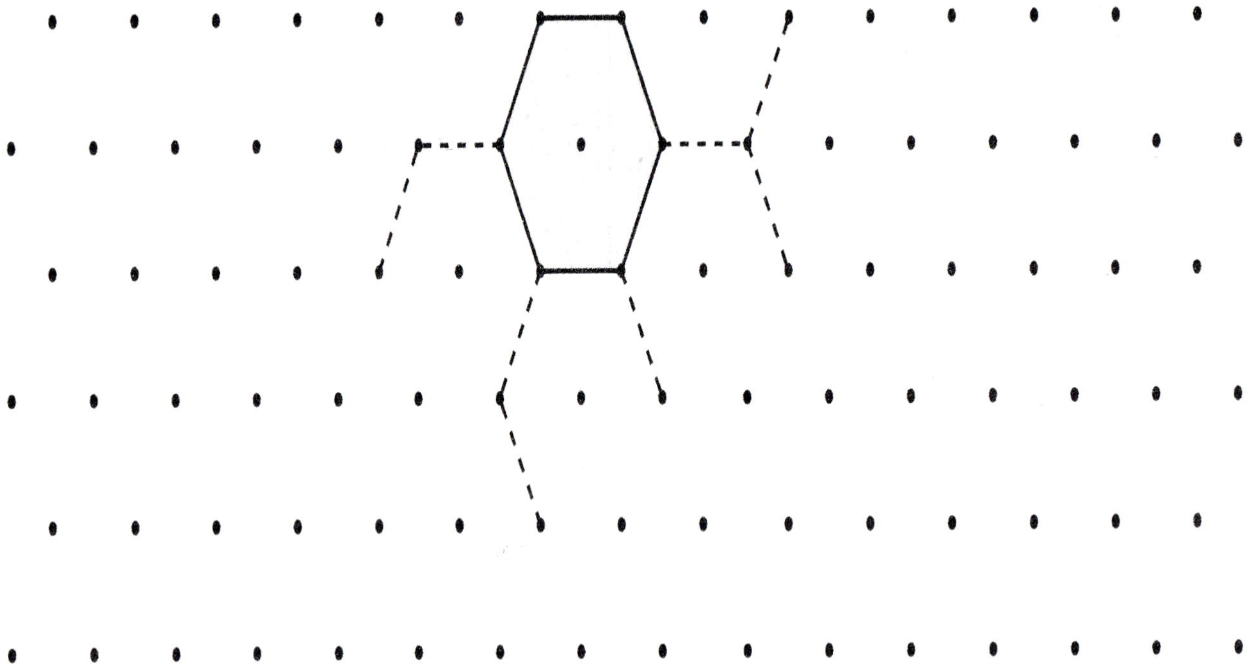

**2.** a. Nishu folded a piece of paper like this. Then he cut off one corner and opened it flat.

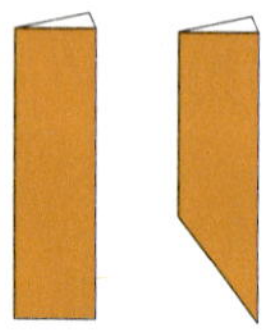

Colour in the shape he made.

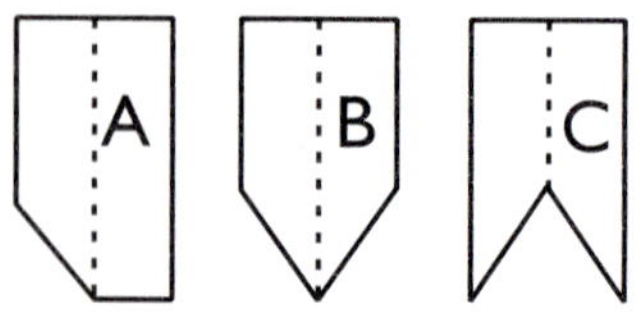


b. Ishu folded his paper, cut out a different piece and opened it out flat.

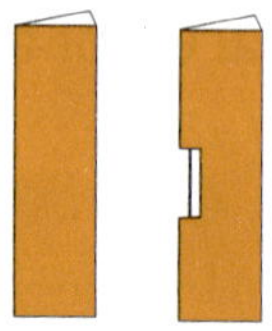

Colour in the shape he made.

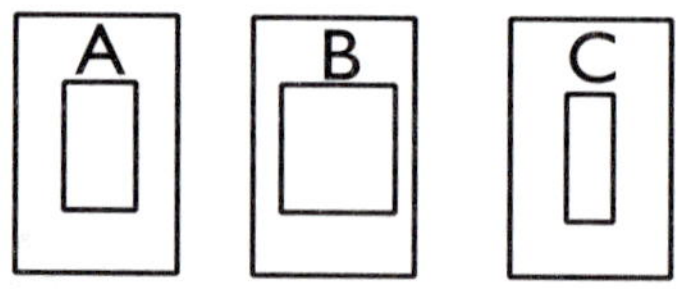

Grade ☐

# ACTIVITY SHEET 47

**1.** Sort out these objects according to the shape they most look like.

a. tennis ball
b. pencil
c. soup tin
d. stack of one rupee coin
e. orange
f. a power pole
g. volcano
h. length of a wire
i. witch's hat
j. marble
k. sharp pencil point
l. world globe

| Cone | Cylinder | Sphere |
|---|---|---|
| | | |

**2.** Toy Sale

Rs 50.00

Rs 85.00

3 for Rs 120.00

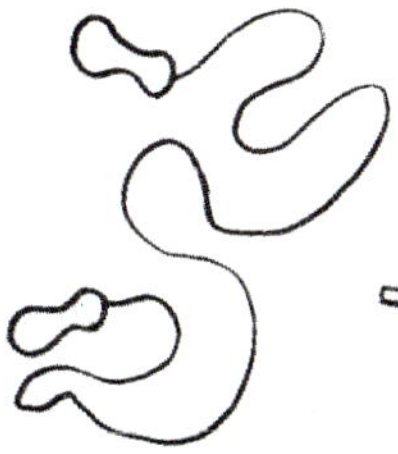

Rs 45.00

Rs 125.00

a. What is the total cost of:

a car and a boat ______ a skipping rope and a boat ______

a drum and 3 books ______ a car and a skipping rope ______

b. How much change from Rs 500 if you buy

a boat and a drum ______ 3 books and a drum ______

c. What is the cost of

1 fairy tale book ______ 6 drums ______

# ACTIVITY SHEET 48

Grade ☐

**1.** Answer the following.

a. Write the largest possible number with four digits. ______

b. Priya had 10 pets. She had cats, parrots and fish. Altogether they had 30 legs. How many of each pet did she own?

cats ______ parrots ______ fish ______

c. Write the next 6 squared numbers.

4, 9, 16, 25, ______, ______, ______, ______, ______, ______

d. If 139 is divided by 4, what is the remainder? ______

e. Add 3 to 157 then divide by 7. What is the remainder? ______

**2.** How many 250 mL cups are needed to fill a

a. 1 L bucket ______ b. 3 L bucket ______ c. 5 L bucket ______

**3.** John's car travels 40 km on 1 litre of fuel. Fuel costs Rs 50 per litre. How much would it cost to travel:

a. 20 km ______ b. 60 km ______

c. 100 km ______ d. 350 km ______

**4.** How many minutes from

a. 5:26 a.m. to 5:58 a.m ______ b. 10:49 p.m to 11:23 p.m. ______

c. 8:06 a.m. to 9:15 a.m. ______ d. 11:31 p.m. to 1:16 a.m. ______

e. 11:16 a.m to 2:14 p.m. ______ f. 12:00 noon to 2:14 p.m. ______

**5.** Sunita bought a pen that costs Rs 10.20 and stamps that cost Rs 3.25. The total cost is close to

a. Rs 14 b. Rs 13 c. Rs 15

**6.** Dhruv wants to buy a toy car which costs Rs 45.50. He has one 20-rupee note and a 5-rupee note. How much more money does he need? ______

Grade

# ACTIVITY SHEET 49

**1.** Eight books costs Rs 480. Find the cost of

a. 1 book ______

b. 6 books ______

**2.** Six pineapples cost Rs 240. Find the cost of

a. 1 pineapple ______

b. 8 pineapples ______

**3.** A car uses 2 litres of fuel to travel 80 km. How far can it travel on:

a. 21 L ______  b. 35 L ______

**4.** A car uses 8 litres of fuel to travel 640 km. How many litres are needed to travel:

a. 24 km _____  b. 160 km _____

**5.** a. Read the pictorial representation and answer the following questions.
What was the Civets population in

1900 ______

1800 ______

1990 ______

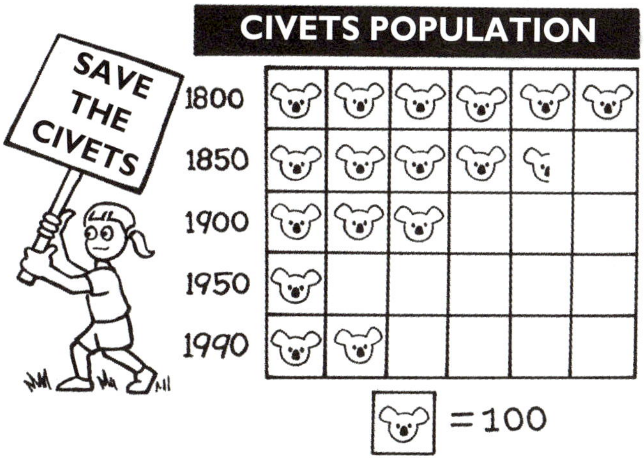


b. What was the difference in population between 1850 and 1950? ______

c. By how many times was the population in 1800 greater than the population in

1900 ______  1950 ______  1990 ______

**4.** Write the correct unit of measure.

a.

200 _____

b.

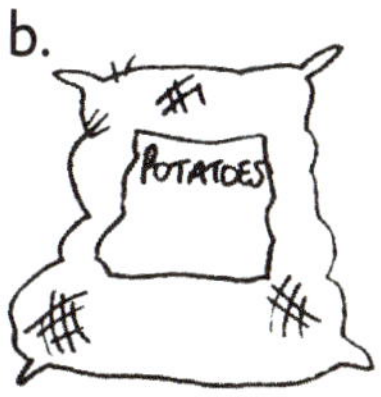


10 _____

c.

1.5 _____

d.

1 _____

# ACTIVITY SHEET 50

Grade

**1.** Answer the following.

a. Which is larger, $\frac{5}{10}$ or $\frac{39}{10}$? ______

b. Average of 21, 22, 24 and 25 is ______

c. Is 112 a multiple of 3? (yes/no) ______

d. 4095 + 11 + 10 + 0 = ______

e. Continue 214, 225, 237, 250, 264, ____, ____, ____, ____, ____, ____, ____, ____

f. A boy was born in 1983. How old will he be in 2000? ______

**2.** Show each time on the clock face.

a. b. c. d. e.

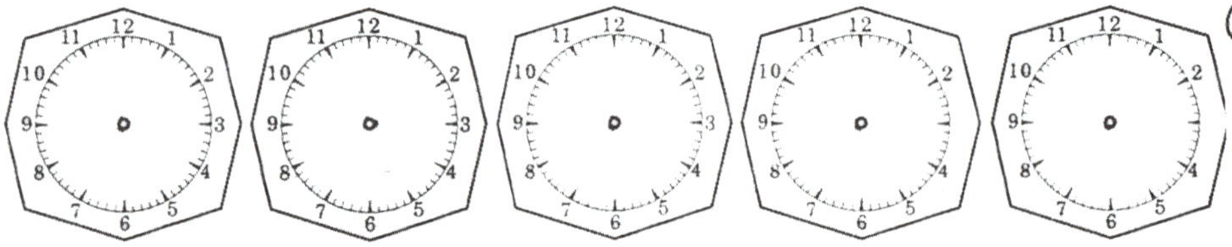

| a. | b. | c. | d. | e. |
|---|---|---|---|---|
| 16:20 | 09:45 | 19:35 | 23:30 | 03:15 |

**3.** Write each time in 24-hour clock time.

a. b. c. d. e.

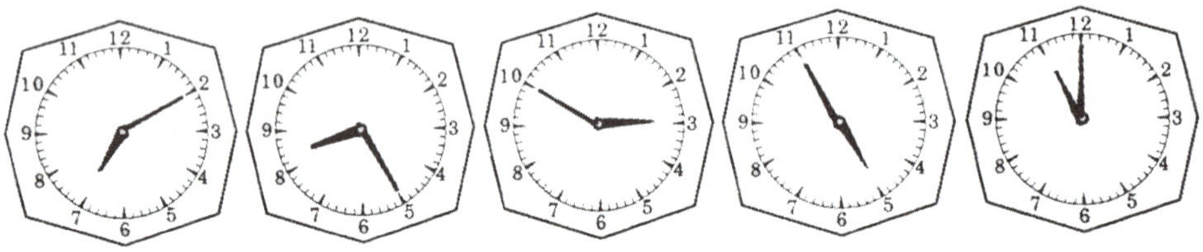

| a. | b. | c. | d. | e. |
|---|---|---|---|---|
| a.m. | p.m. | p.m. | a.m. | p.m. |
| | | | | |

**4.** A book contains 405 pages. How many pages are there in 25 books? ________

5. A girl saves Rs 550 each month. How much money will she save in 3 years? ________

Grade

# ACTIVITY SHEET 51

**1.** Add two numbers side by side to get the one above. Complete each pyramid.

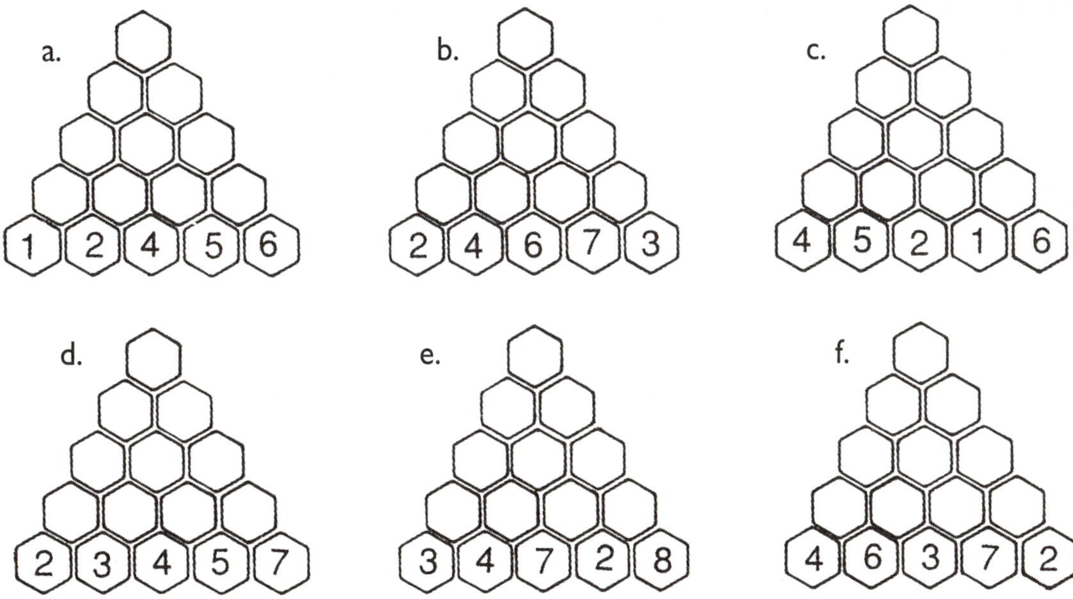

**2.**

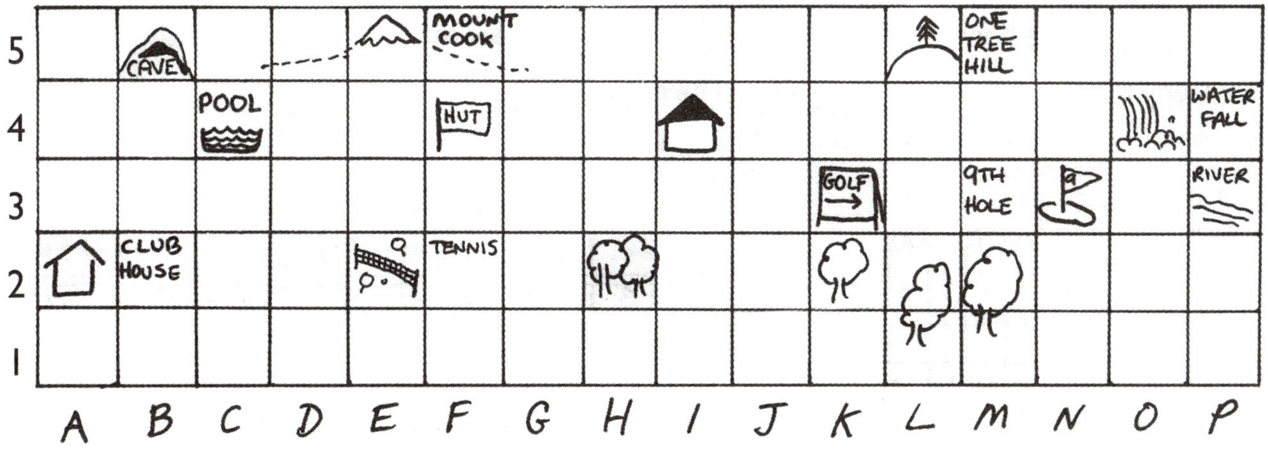


a. What are the coordinates of:

b. What is located at:

K3 ______ E2 ______

C4 ______ O4 ______

N3 ______ B5 ______

# ACTIVITY SHEET 52

Grade

**1.** These shapes have been formed using match-sticks. How many match-sticks are needed to make a line of

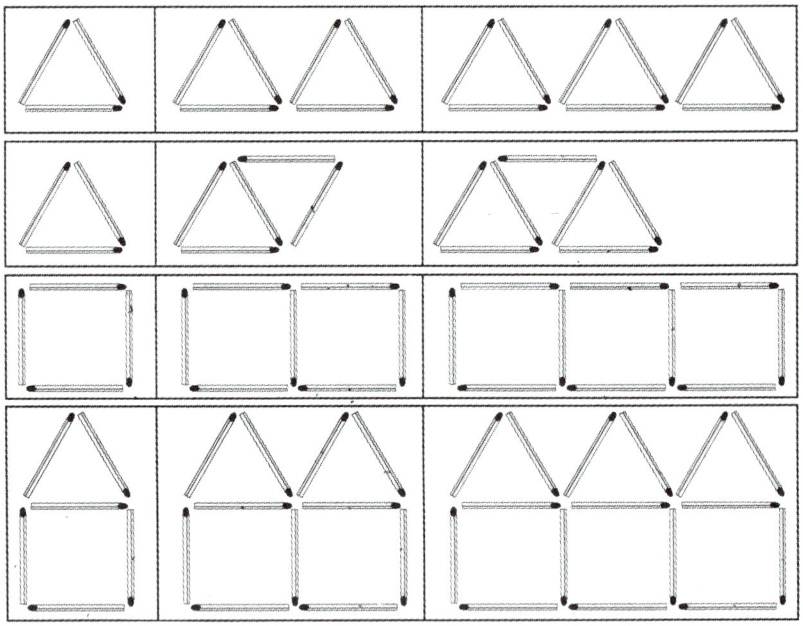

a. 5 triangles ______

b. 100 triangles ______

c. 6 triangles ______

d. 80 triangles ______

e. 8 squares ______

f. 100 squares ______

g. 10 houses ______

h. 80 houses ______

**2.** Some of the multiples of 2 are: 2, 4, 6, 8, 10, 12, 14, 16, 18, 20.
The unit digits are 2, 4, 6, 8, 0.

When joined in order, these make a unit digit pattern.

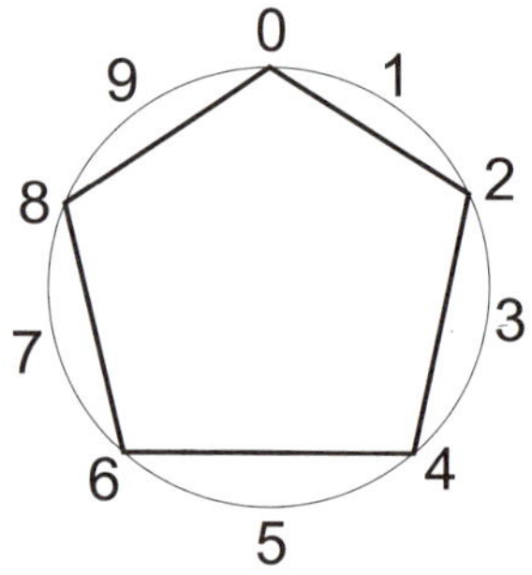


Draw the unit digit pattern for the multiples of 6, 4, 3 and 8.

a.

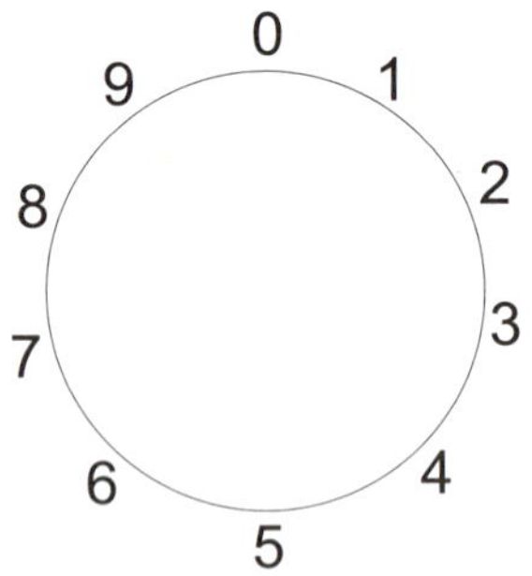


6

b.

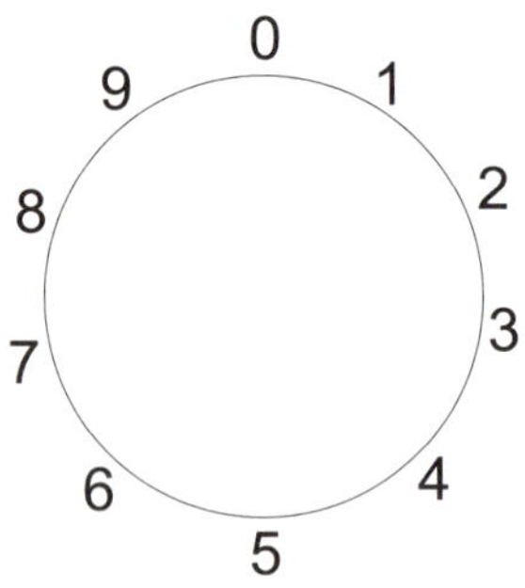


4

c.

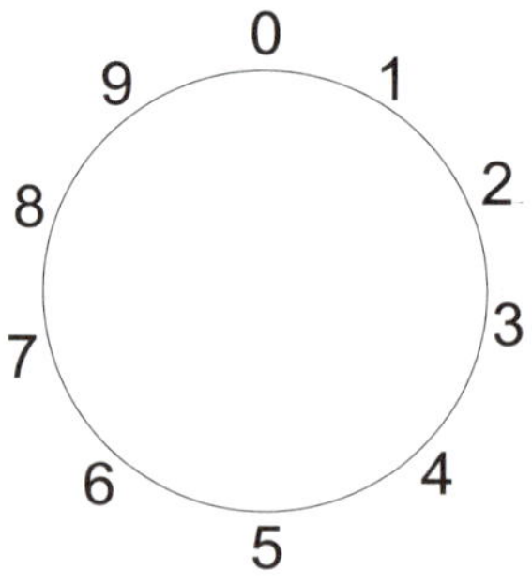


3

d.

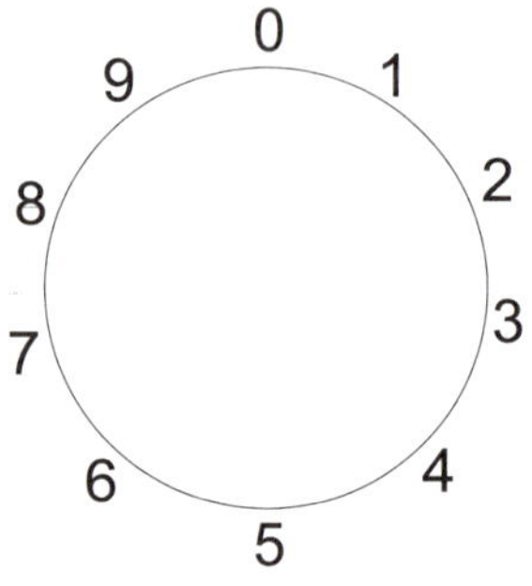


8

Grade

# ACTIVITY SHEET 53

**1.** Colour the cube that matches each net.

a.

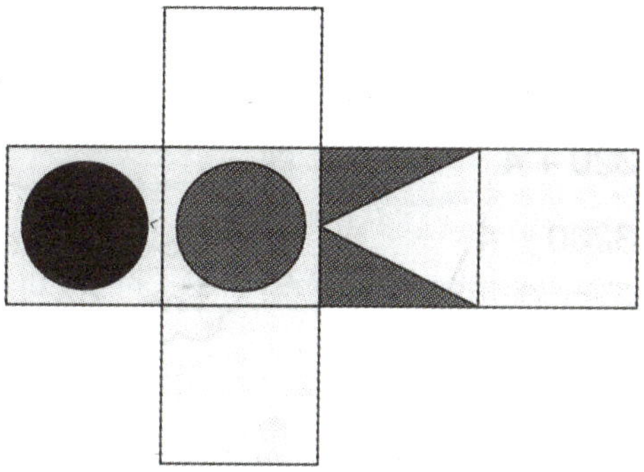

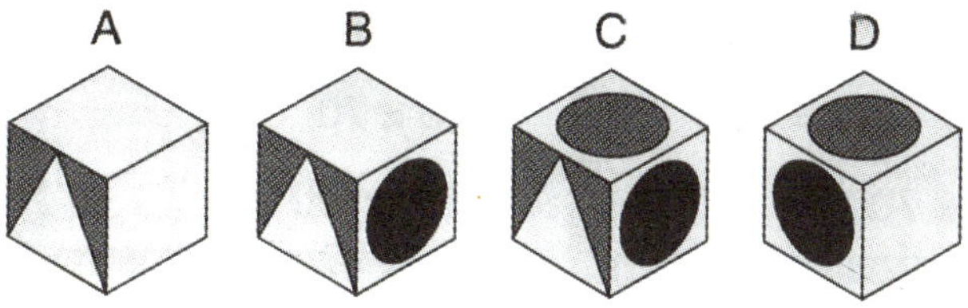


b.

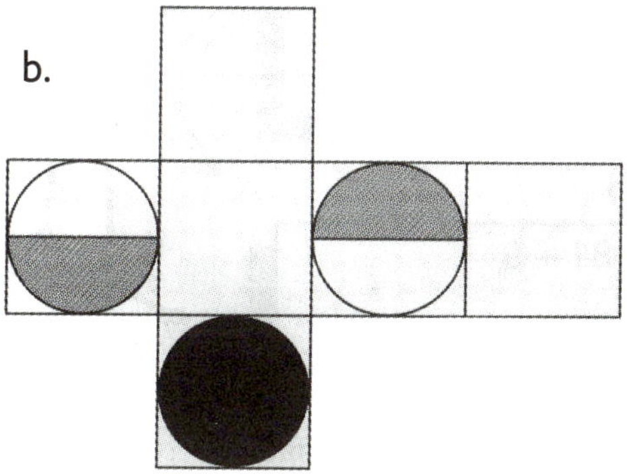

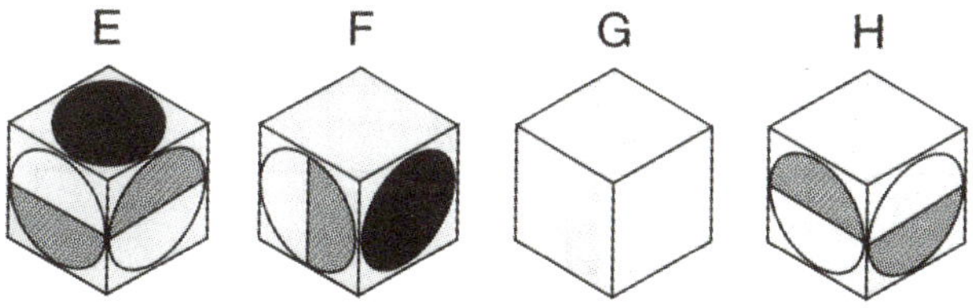


**2.** Complete each table. One has been done for you.

a.

| | |
|---|---|
| 3 × 7 | = 21 |
| 3 × 70 | = 210 |
| 3 × 700 | = 2100 |

b.

| | |
|---|---|
| 8 × 7 | = ______ |
| 8 × 70 | = ______ |
| 8 × 700 | = ______ |

c.

| | |
|---|---|
| 32 ÷ 4 | = ______ |
| 320 ÷ 4 | = ______ |
| 3200 ÷ 4 | = ______ |

d.

| | |
|---|---|
| 5 × 9 | = ______ |
| 5 × 90 | = ______ |
| 5 × 900 | = ______ |

e.

| | |
|---|---|
| 9 × 6 | = ______ |
| 9 × 60 | = ______ |
| 9 × 600 | = ______ |

f.

| | |
|---|---|
| 40 ÷ 8 | = ______ |
| 400 ÷ 8 | = ______ |
| 4000 ÷ 8 | = ______ |

g.

| | |
|---|---|
| 6 × 8 | = ______ |
| 6 × 80 | = ______ |
| 6 × 800 | = ______ |

h.

| | |
|---|---|
| 7 × 9 | = ______ |
| 7 × 90 | = ______ |
| 7 × 900 | = ______ |

i.

| | |
|---|---|
| 81 ÷ 9 | = ______ |
| 810 ÷ 9 | = ______ |
| 8100 ÷ 9 | = ______ |

# ACTIVITY SHEET 54

Grade

**1.** Write the unit of measurement you would use to find.

a. the length of a blue whale ______

b. the area of your bedroom ______

c. the weight of a child ______

d. the area of your desktop ______

e. the volume of milk in a bottle ______

f. the weight of a pack of biscuits ______

g. the volume of water in a swimming pool ______

h. the distance from Delhi to Kolkata ______

i. the volume of a liquid in a medicine cup ______

**2.** There are various shapes in this hexagon. Find and colour one of each type.

a. triangle: red

b. hexagon: orange

c. square: yellow

d. rectangle: green

e. rhombus: blue

f. parallelogram: purple

**3.** Trace over each dotted line once, without lifting your pencil from the paper. Do not retrace any line. Start at the arrow.

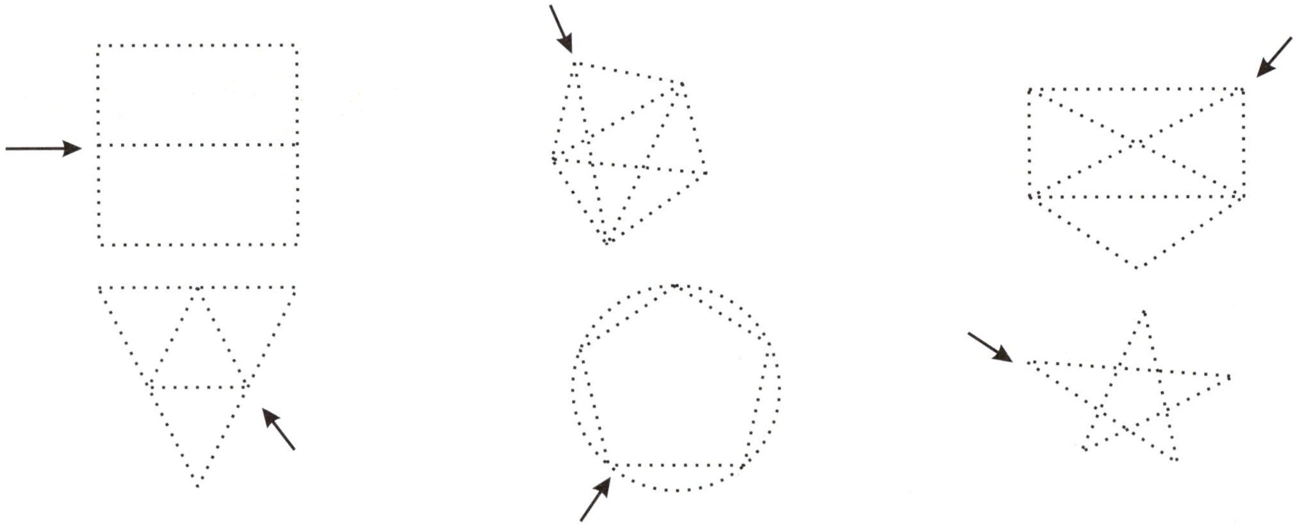

Grade

# ACTIVITY SHEET 55

**1.** Matthew collected cans and graphed the total at the end of each day for 14 days.

a. How many cans did he have at the end of

day 4 ______

day 7 ______

day 13 ______

b. On which day did he cash in his cans ______

c. How many cans were collected on day 11? ______

d. On what day had he collected a total of

20 cans ______ 30 cans ______ 50 cans ______

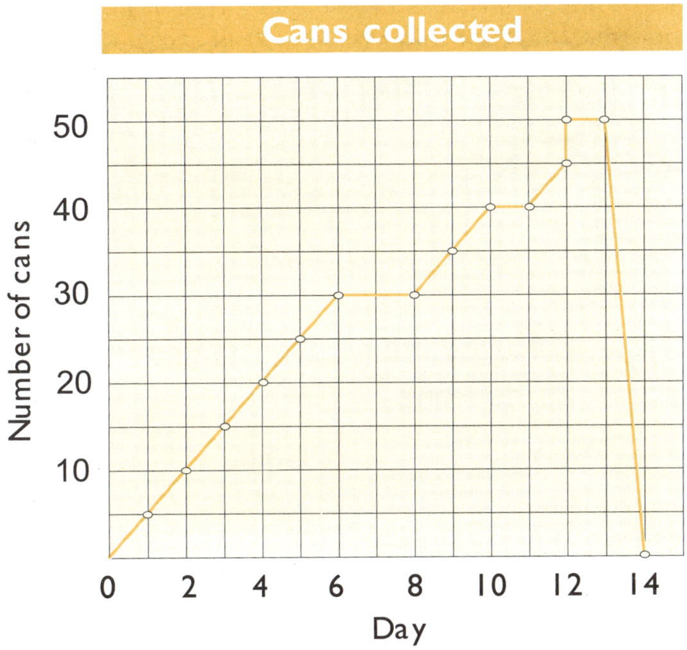


**2.** Study the table and answer the following questions.

| | Fri | Sat | Sun | Mon |
|---|---|---|---|---|
| 11:00 | 24 °C | 26 °C | 27 °C | 17 °C |
| 1:00 | 28 °C | 30 °C | 33 °C | 20 °C |
| 3:00 | 28 °C | 29 °C | 31 °C | 18 °C |
| 5:00 | 23 °C | 26 °C | 23 °C | 16 °C |

a. Which day had the highest temperature? ______

b. Which day had the greatest difference in temperature? ______

c. What was the coolest temperature? ______

d. Which day had a cool change? ______

e. Are these temperatures for day and night? ______

f. The highest temperature is at 1:00. Is this unusual? ______

g. Would these temperatures be more suitable for a town in Himachal Pradesh or a town in Rajasthan? ______

# ACTIVITY SHEET 56

Grade ☐

**1.** These cats have been made from playdoh.

Each toy cat has a mass of 120 g.

a. Calculate the number that could be made from:

250 g ______ 500 g ______

b. Calculate the weight of

5 cats ______ 8 cats ______

**2.** Puja was born in 1997. When she turns 30, her uncle Shyam will be 65 years old. When was Shyam born? ______

**3.** Circle those with the same value as

| | | | | | |
|---|---|---|---|---|---|
| a. | **35 x 50** | 55 x 45 | 35 x 75 | 875 x 20 | 350 x 5 |
| b. | **45 ÷ 9** | 63 ÷ 7 | 899 + 1 | 30 x 30 | 1029 – 1020 |
| c. | **80 x 90** | 800 x 90 | 900 x 40 | 720 x 10 | 900 x 8 |
| d. | **320 ÷ 2** | 80 x 2 | 40 x 4 | 180 – 120 | 100 + 64 |

**4.** Convert 20 minutes before 9:10 p.m. into 24 hour clock time. ______

**5.** Fill in the blanks.

a. 7 years 9 months + 6 years 11 months = ______ years ______ months

b. Now give your answer in weeks and days. ______ weeks ______ days

Grade

# ACTIVITY SHEET 57

**1.** Write the numbers.

a. 9,00,000 + 60,000 + 4000 + 800 + 20 + 9 = ____________________

b. 7,00,000 + 30,000 + 8000 + 700 + 40 + 0 = ____________________

c. 8,00,000 + 20,000 + 2000 + 900 + 60 + 4 = ____________________

d. 9,00,000 + 60,000 + 0 + 900 + 20 + 7 = ____________________

e. 5,00,000 + 20,000 + 3000 + 200 + 0 + 2 = ____________________

f. 7,00,000 + 50,000 + 2000 + 0 + 50 + 20 = ____________________

**2.** Fill in the blanks with the correct sign (<, > or =)

a. 9,71,234 ________ 9,24,134

b. 9,38,260 ________ 9,40,259

c. 7,91,326 ________ 7,91,246

d. 2,76,310 ________ 2,12,001

e. 8,67,104 ________ 8,10,402

f. 5,00,651 ________ 2,00,876

g. 6,06,312 ________ 5,06,315

h. 8,34,795 ________ 8,36,917

i. 3,01,723 ________ 2,03,934

j. 5,20,220 ________ 5,09,220

**3.** Write the successor and predecessors of the following numbers:

| | Predecessor | Number | Successor |
|---|---|---|---|
| a. | | 9,02,209 | |
| b. | | 5,40,610 | |
| c. | | 3,23,500 | |
| d. | | 99,999 | |
| e. | | 9,99,998 | |
| f. | | 45,699 | |

# ACTIVITY SHEET 58

Grade ☐

**1.** Fill in the blanks with >, < or = sign.

a. $\frac{1}{6} \bigcirc \frac{3}{6}$  b. $\frac{5}{7} \bigcirc \frac{1}{7}$  c. $\frac{14}{19} \bigcirc \frac{13}{19}$  d. $\frac{9}{12} \bigcirc \frac{3}{12}$

e. $\frac{8}{25} \bigcirc \frac{19}{25}$  f. $\frac{8}{11} \bigcirc \frac{7}{11}$  g. $\frac{5}{20} \bigcirc \frac{2}{20}$  h. $\frac{5}{2} \bigcirc \frac{1}{2}$

**2.** Write the following in increasing order.

a. $\frac{2}{13}, \frac{5}{13}, \frac{1}{13}, \frac{9}{13}, \frac{4}{13},$ ____ ____ ____ ____ ____

b. $\frac{4}{11}, \frac{6}{11}, \frac{5}{11}, \frac{2}{11}, \frac{3}{11},$ ____ ____ ____ ____ ____

c. $\frac{7}{16}, \frac{13}{16}, \frac{9}{16}, \frac{15}{16}, \frac{5}{16},$ ____ ____ ____ ____ ____

d. $\frac{2}{4}, \frac{1}{4}, \frac{4}{4}, \frac{3}{4}, \frac{6}{4},$ ____ ____ ____ ____ ____

**3.** Write the following in decreasing order.

a. $\frac{3}{10}, \frac{7}{10}, \frac{5}{10}, \frac{8}{10}, \frac{2}{10},$ ____ ____ ____ ____ ____

b. $\frac{6}{17}, \frac{9}{17}, \frac{10}{17}, \frac{15}{17}, \frac{8}{17},$ ____ ____ ____ ____ ____

c. $\frac{3}{12}, \frac{7}{12}, \frac{1}{12}, \frac{11}{12}, \frac{4}{12},$ ____ ____ ____ ____ ____

d. $\frac{5}{8}, \frac{3}{8}, \frac{7}{8}, \frac{6}{8}, \frac{8}{8},$ ____ ____ ____ ____ ____

Grade

# ACTIVITY SHEET 59

1. Find the least four-digit number that can be formed using the digits 6, 0, 3, 1 only once. __________

2. Find the fifth number of the series 1200, 1204, 1208, 1212. __________

3. How many points are there in a straight line? __________

4. (7 x 8) – 26 = __________

5. Find the number of oranges in 12 dozens. __________

6. If 8 kg potatoes cost Rs 120, find the cost of 1 kg potatoes. __________

7. How many litres in 7000 ml? __________

8. Find the sum of the first five multiples of 3? __________

9. How many seconds are there in 5 minutes? __________

10. How many minutes are there in 3 hours? __________

11. Write at least six problems with the answers as 2007.

For example, find the difference of 4007 and 2000.

a. ______________________________

b. ______________________________

c. ______________________________

d. ______________________________

e. ______________________________

f. ______________________________

# ACTIVITY SHEET 60

Grade

1. A blackboard is 20 m in length and 14 m in breadth. Find its perimeter and area.

   a. Perimeter ______ b. Area ______

2. Write the numbers.

   a. Forty million thirty-four thousand and seventy-eight ________

   b. Nine hundred twenty-five thousand three hundred and fourteen ________

   c. Nine crores twelve lakhs four thousand and eighty-two ________

   d. Fifty three lakhs eleven thousand four hundred and three ________

3. Count the squares and find the area of the given figures. Each square is 1 cm in length and breadth.

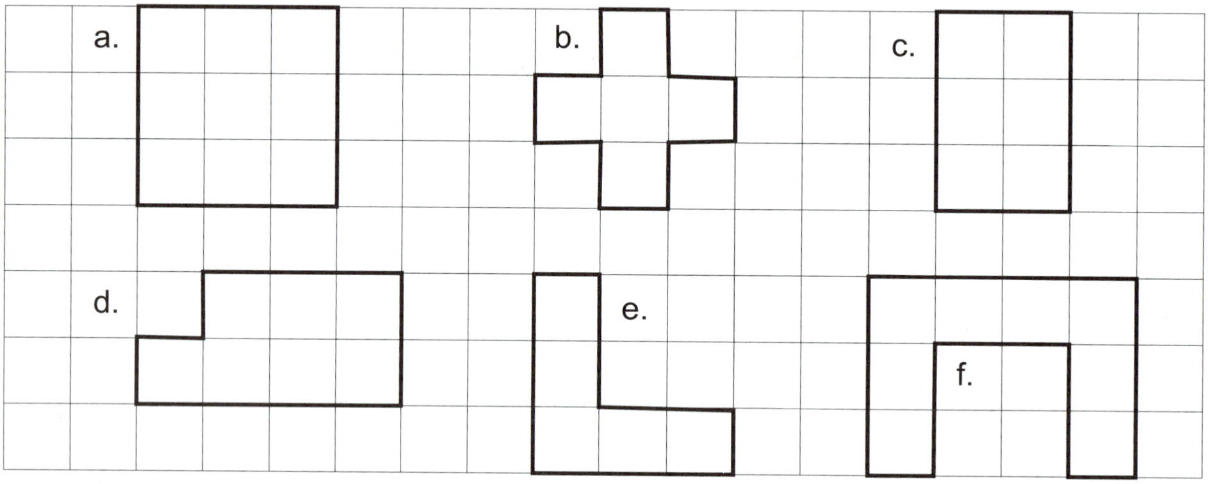


a. ________ b. ________ c. ________

d. ________ e. ________ f. ________

4. Assume each square to be a rectangle of breadth 1 cm and length 2 cm. Now find the area of each figure.

a. ________ b. ________ c. ________

d. ________ e. ________ f. ________

Grade ☐

# ACTIVITY SHEET 61

**1.** Help Tina buy the correct square-metres of carpet required to cover the floors of all the rooms of her house. The dimensions of different rooms are given below.

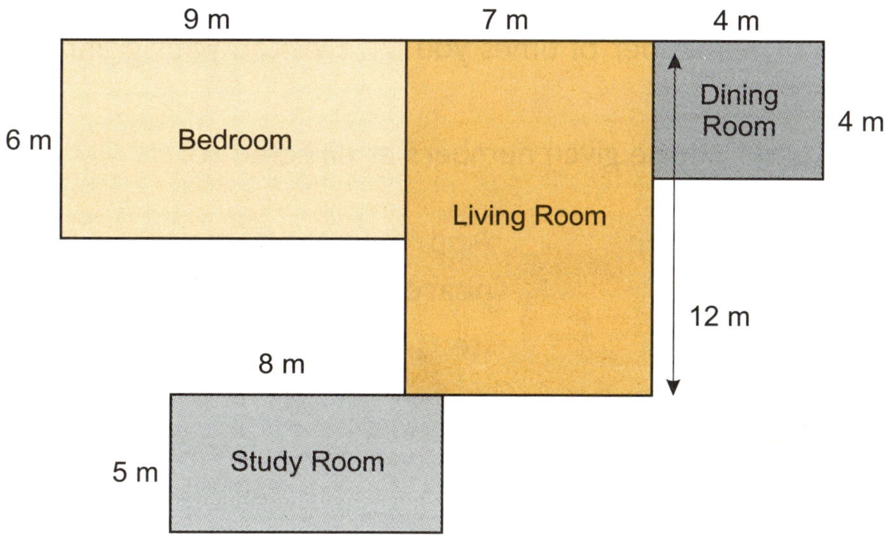


a. Carpet required for the bedroom = ______

b. Carpet required for the living room = ______

c. Carpet required for the study room = ______

d. Carpet required for the dining room = ______

e. Total square-metre of the carpet required = ______

**2.** If the cost of carpet is Rs 5 per square-metres, then find the total cost. ______

**3.** How much money will Tina save, if she buys the carpets from a sale which offers it at Rs 4 per square-metres? ______

# ACTIVITY SHEET 62

Grade

**1.** Estimate the following.

a. The number of guests invited to a small dinner party at your place. ______

b. The population of the city you are living in. ______

c. The total number of students in your school. ______

d. The time you will take to answer all the question on this page. ______

e. The number of times you have visited your grandparents' place since birth. ______

**2.** Round off the given numbers as directed to.

| Number | Approximated to the nearest | Rounded off number |
|---|---|---|
| 96451 | tens | |
| 96451 | hundreds | |
| 96451 | thousands | |

**3.** Rounded off and estimated sum of 53 and 191 is 50 + 200 = 250. Similarly the estimated difference of 478 and 290 is 500 – 300 = 200. Now estimate sum or difference of the following.

a. 28 + 219 = ______

b. 326 + 640 = ______

c. 896 + 208 = ______

d. 503 + 994 = ______

e. 340 – 67 = ______

f. 1216 – 782 = ______

g. 295 + 886 = ______

h. 763 – 436 = ______

**4.** Simplify:

a. 9419 + 5001 – 2004 = ______

b. 2940 ÷ 30 = ______

c. 5670 ÷ 20 = ______

d. 8000 ÷ 20 = ______

e. 729 ÷ 29 = ______

f. (8370 – 4190) + 3150 + 2140 = ______

g. (4973 – 2914) + (4210 + 940) = ______

Grade ☐

# ACTIVITY SHEET 63

**1.** Frame at least five word problems involving subtraction, addition, multiplication and division. Three examples have been given.

a. The cost of 2 books is Rs 100. Find the cost of 20 books.

b. What number should be added to 400 to get 1400?

c. A train travels 50 km in 1 hour. How far will it travel in 20 hours?

d. ______________________________

______________________________

e. ______________________________

______________________________

f. ______________________________

______________________________

g. ______________________________

______________________________

h. ______________________________

______________________________

**2.** 4, 5, 6 are next-door numbers. Use next-door numbers to make these true.

a. ◯ + ◯ + ◯ = 9

b. ◯ + ◯ + ◯ = 24

c. ◯ + ◯ + ◯ = 30

d. ◯ + ◯ + ◯ = 33

e. ◯ + ◯ + ◯ + ◯ = 18

f. ◯ + ◯ + ◯ + ◯ + ◯ = 20

# ACTIVITY SHEET 64

Grade

**1.** Round off the numbers and estimate the product. For example, the estimated product of 11 and 63 is 10 × 60 = 600. By approximating both the numbers to the nearest tens we get 10 and 60. Therefore the estimated product will be 600.

Now round off the following numbers and estimate their product.

a. 56 × 82 = ______  b. 21 × 117 = ______

c. 7 × 487 = ______  d. 98 × 489 = ______

e. 206 × 315 = ______  f. 72 x 43 = ______

♦ Working rule for multipliers like 9, 99 and 999.
Place as many zeros to the right of the multiplicand as in the number of nines in the multiplier. From the number so obtained, subtract the multiplicand to get the difference. For example,

$$
\begin{aligned}
73 \times 99 &= (73 \times 100) - (73 \times 1) \\
&= 7300 - 73 \\
&= 7227
\end{aligned}
$$

Multiply:

a. 48 × 9 = ______  b. 576 × 99 = ______

c. 642 × 99 = ______  d. 85 × 999 = ______

e. 115 × 99 = ______

**2.** Draw all lines of symmetry.

a.

b.
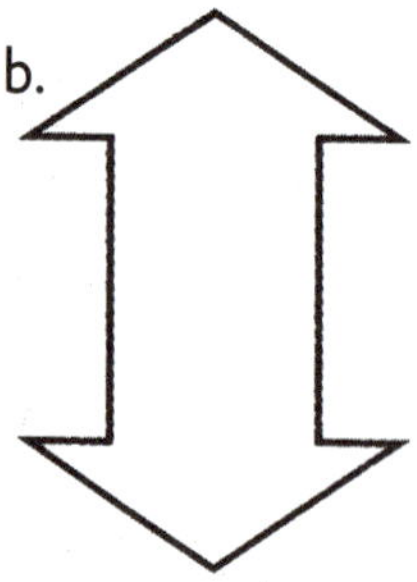

c.

d.
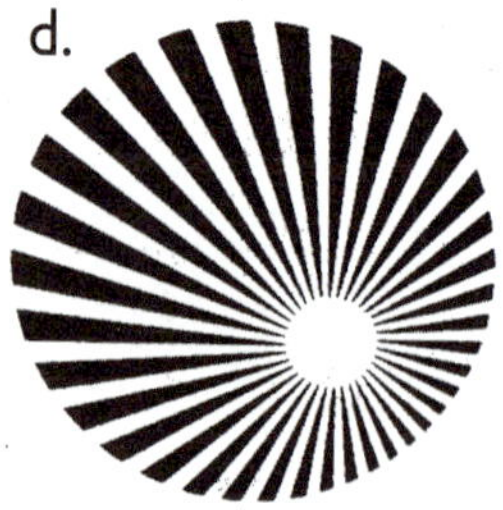

Grade ☐

# ACTIVITY SHEET 65

**1.** Write any five multiples of the following numbers.

| Number | Multiples |
|---|---|
| 2 | |
| 3 | |
| 5 | |
| 6 | |
| 10 | |
| 12 | |
| 19 | |
| 20 | |

**2.** Write any five factors of the following numbers.

| Number | Factors |
|---|---|
| 50 | |
| 100 | |
| 150 | |
| 200 | |
| 800 | |
| 1000 | |
| 240 | |
| 420 | |
| 500 | |
| 630 | |

**3.** Write three more facts for each. One has been done for you.

a. $48 \div 6 = 8$ <u>$64 \div 8 = 8$</u>, ______________, ______________

b. $6 \times 9 = 54$ ______________, ______________, ______________

# ACTIVITY SHEET 66

Grade

**1.** Add or Subtract the following. One has been done for you.

a. $\frac{6}{11} - \frac{2}{11} = \frac{6-2}{11} = \frac{4}{11}$

b. $\frac{7}{9} + \frac{3}{9} =$ ______

c. $\frac{4}{17} - \frac{6}{17} =$ ______

d. $\frac{9}{16} - \frac{4}{16} =$ ______

e. $\frac{12}{19} + \frac{8}{19} =$ ______

f. $\frac{12}{19} - \frac{8}{19} =$ ______

**2.** Write any 5 equivalent fractions for the following. One has been done for you.

a. $\frac{1}{3} = \frac{2}{6} = \frac{3}{9} = \frac{4}{12} = \frac{5}{15} = \frac{6}{18}$

b. $\frac{3}{5} =$

c. $\frac{1}{2} =$

d. $\frac{1}{5} =$

e. $\frac{1}{4} =$

f. $\frac{4}{9} =$

**3.** Here is a map of some city-streets.

a. Draw this path on the map.

Start at the car park

travel 5 blocks north; then 3 blocks east;

then 1 block south; then 2 blocks west;

then 1 block east;

b. Where did your path end? __________

c. How long is your path? __________

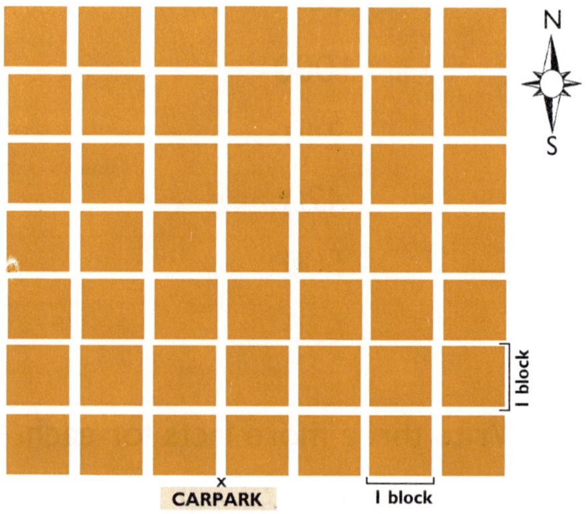


**1 block = 1 km**

Grade

# ACTIVITY SHEET 67

Test your speed.

How many can you complete in each set in two minutes?

| Score |
| --- |
| |

**1.** a. $3 \times 10 =$ ______
b. $10^2 =$ ______ c. $50 \div 10 =$ ______ d. $7 \times 10 =$ ______
e. $9 \times 10 =$ ______ f. $45 \div 5 =$ ______ g. $40 \div 10 =$ ______
h. $5 \times 10 =$ ______ i. $8 \times 10 =$ ______ j. $60 \div 10 =$ ______
k. $100 \div 10 =$ ______ l. $4 \times 10 =$ ______ m. $2 \times 10 =$ ______
n. $30 \div 10 =$ ______ o. $70 \div 10 =$ ______ p. $6 \times 10 =$ ______
q. $10 \times 1 =$ ______ r. $20 \div 10 =$ ______ s. $90 \div 10 =$ ______
t. $10 \times 10 =$ ______ u. $10 \times 0 =$ ______

**2.** a. $4 \times 4 =$ ______ b. $28 \div 4 =$ ______ c. $40 \div 4 =$ ______
d. $6 \times 4 =$ ______ e. $2 \times 4 =$ ______ f. $4^2 =$ ______
g. $8 \times 4 =$ ______ h. $24 \div 4 =$ ______ i. $5 \times 4 =$ ______
j. $100 \times 4 =$ ______ k. $16 \div 4 =$ ______ l. $20 \div 4 =$ ______
m. $3 \times 4 =$ ______ n. $7 \times 4 =$ ______ o. $25 \times 4 =$ ______
p. $32 \div 4 =$ ______ q. $9 \times 4 =$ ______ r. $36 \div 6 =$ ______
s. $4 + 4 + 3 + 2 =$ ______

**3.** a. $6 \times 8 =$ ______ b. $80 \div 8 =$ ______ c. $24 \div 8 =$ ______
d. $4 \times 8 =$ ______ e. $7 \times 8 =$ ______ f. $40 \div 8 =$ ______
g. $42 \div 6 =$ ______ h. $24 \div 4 =$ ______ i. $4^2 =$ ______
j. $100 \times 4 =$ ______ k. $16 \div 4 =$ ______ l. $20 \div 4 =$ ______
m. $3 \times 4 =$ ______ n. $48 \div 8 =$ ______ o. $32 \div 8 =$ ______
p. $3 \times 8 =$ ______ q. $4 \times 8 =$ ______ r. $56 \div 8 =$ ______
s. $72 \div 8 =$ ______

# Quiz - Time 3

Time: 15 minutes

Score ________

1. Write $\frac{3}{7}$ in words. ________________________
2. If a circular shape is divided into 5 equal parts and 3 parts are shaded then what fraction is shaded? ______
3. Round off 9536 to the nearest hundred. ______
4. The sum of 5210 and 7220 is = ______
5. The difference between 7520 and 5210 = ______
6. The 15th letter of the alphabet is ______
7. Round off 16621 to the nearest thousand. ______
8. Which is smaller, three-eighths or five-eighths? ______
9. How many fingers have 45 girls? ______
10. Is 65169 bigger than 65196? ______
11. Place value of 7 in 47301 is ______
12. Thousand in 49136 is ______
13. Rs 160 shared by 4. How much each gets? ______
14. Roman numeral for 78 ______
15. Which is larger, one whole or ninety-six hundredths? ______
16. The sum of two prime numbers is 20. What are they? a. ______ b. ______
17. List the multiples of 4 between 30 and 50. ________________________
18. Circle the numbers, divisible by 3.

    21 34 73 99 123
19. How many quarters in 8? ______
20. Are 125 and 130 multiples of 5? ______
21. Place value of 2 in 29631 is ______
22. 20000 + 8000 + 600 + 50 + 4 = ______
23. If 1o'clock is 1300 hours then 4 o'clock is ______ hours.